RUDOLF STEINER (1861–1925) called his spiritual philosophy 'anthroposophy', meaning 'wisdom of the human being'. As a highly developed seer, he based his work on direct knowledge and perception of spiritual dimensions. He initiated a modern and universal 'science of spirit', accessible to anyone willing to exercise clear and unprejudiced thinking.

From his spiritual investigations Steiner provided suggestions for the renewal of many activities, including education (both general and special), agriculture, medicine, economics, architecture, science, philosophy, religion and the arts. Today there are thousands of schools, clinics, farms and other organizations involved in practical work based on his principles. His many published works feature his research into the spiritual nature of the human being, the evolution of the world and humanity, and methods of personal development. Steiner wrote some 30 books and delivered over 6000 lectures across Europe. In 1924 he founded the General Anthroposophical Society, which today has branches throughout the world.

THE KARMA OF ANTHROPOSOPHY

Rudolf Steiner, the Anthroposophical Society and the Tasks of its Members

RUDOLF STEINER

Compiled and edited by Margaret Jonas and Matthew Barton

RUDOLF STEINER PRESS

Rudolf Steiner Press
Hillside House, The Square
Forest Row, RH18 5ES

www.rudolfsteinerpress.com

Published by Rudolf Steiner Press 2009

Earlier English publications: see Sources section on p. 178

Originally published in German in various volumes of the GA (*Rudolf Steiner Gesamtausgabe* or Collected Works) by Rudolf Steiner Verlag, Dornach. For further information see Sources, p. 178. This authorized translation is published by permission of the Rudolf Steiner Nachlassverwaltung, Dornach

All material has been translated or checked against the original German by Matthew Barton

A catalogue record for this book is available from the British Library

ISBN: 978 185584 219 9

Cover by Andrew Morgan Design
Typeset by DP Photosetting, Neath, West Glamorgan
Printed and bound by Gutenberg Press Ltd., Malta

Contents

Editor's Preface

The lectures and excerpts compiled here do not aim to be an exhaustive account of all that Rudolf Steiner said during 1924, his last year on earth, about the karma of the Anthroposophical Society. However they certainly do reproduce the most salient points he was making, and vividly highlight what he saw as the anthroposophical movement's vital task in renewing civilization and preserving it from the threat of decline. In these lectures and excerpts—here presented in the chronological order in which they were given, and ending with Rudolf Steiner's last address—we can really get a sense of an imminent spiritual battle, of huge forces gathering to fight for the soul of humanity.

A movement is of course only as strong as the sum of its members, and their sincere engagement and collaborative participation. To waken the members of the Anthroposophical Society to the dimensions of their task, Steiner felt it essential for them to recognize each other in a profound sense: to understand the many different karmic threads from which the movement is woven. Such recognition—of difference as much as unity—can give the strength of diversity which, if unconscious and unrecognized, would easily otherwise sunder people. In other words, Steiner saw the unity of the Anthroposophical Society not as something in any way imposed or artificial, but as rooted instead in its members' perception and understanding of their own deepest impulses in past lives and in the world of spirit between these lives.

This offers us a really striking panorama, in which we are

compelled to broaden our narrow vision of life in general and anthroposophical endeavour in particular, and see the Anthroposophical Society not as a small backwater promoting hopeful but insignificant ventures, more or less drowned out by the pouring torrents of the mainstream, but—to use a different metaphor—as the live yeast that can set all culture rising.

Steiner was at pains to emphasize that reflections on karma involve great subtlety and complexity, along with the need for a sense of deep responsibility. There is inevitable repetition here, since these lectures were given to a range of different audiences. Yet on each occasion Steiner approaches the same or similar aspects from a subtly different perspective, and this is surely one way in which he tried to do justice to the interwoven complexity of his theme.

M.B.

Prelude: The Ghosts of the Past

Extract from a lecture given at the Goetheanum on 4 July 1924

Each of us experiences our personal destiny. But when even two people work together something quite different arises than just fulfilment of each person's separate destiny. Something develops and unfolds between these two people which goes beyond what each individual experiences alone. For ordinary consciousness, the connection between this kind of dynamic between people and what occurs above in the world of spirit is not immediately discernible. Only when sacred, spiritual activity is drawn into the sensory, physical world, when people intentionally transform their physical and sensory deeds so that they become, simultaneously, deeds in the world of spirit, is such a connection created.

And all that occurs between people in this way, in a broader dimension, is something quite different from what each of us experiences as our destiny. Everything which is not individual human destiny but comes about through thinking, sensing, feeling and acting together is connected with what the Seraphim, Cherubim and Thrones do above in the worlds of spirit. And into their deeds flow the deeds wrought through human connections, and in the convergence of separate human lives.

The wider view that opens to the gaze of the initiate is of particular significance here. We gaze upwards and there we see the heavenly consequences of what occurred on earth in the late 70s, the 80s and 90s of the nineteenth century. It is as if a fine, spiritual rain were falling down upon earth, trickling into human souls and urging them to engage in what now arises between people today, as historical consequence one can say.

And in turn we can likewise see how what was done here on earth by human beings in the 70s, 80s and 90s of the last century still lives in vivid thought reflections mediated by the Seraphim, Cherubim and Thrones.

If we understand these things we can have precise insight into the following. When speaking with someone today, you can sense that whatever he says that does not really come through his own emotions or inward impulse, but instead is general opinion and is expressed in this way because he is simply a child of his age, is often connected with people who are no longer alive but lived in the 70s, 80s and 90s of the past century. It is really the case that we can often see someone today as though surrounded by a gathering of spirits who are working upon him but are really only the after-images raining down of what lived in people on earth during the last third of the nineteenth century.

Thus in a real sense you can say that the revenants, the ghosts of a former age, mingle with a later one. This is one of the subtle, general karmic influences which affect things in the world, and which the most occult of occultists often do not consider. Nowadays one often feels like saying to someone who expresses a regurgitated view rather than something that comes from himself, his own personal experience: 'That's just something that's been passed on to you from the last third of the nineteenth century!'

Only in this way can we see life as a whole. And when we examine this age we live in, beginning with the end of the Kali Yuga or dark age, we have to realize how it differs, initially, from all former historical ages. The difference lies in the fact that the human deeds which occurred in the last third of the nineteenth century still exert the greatest imaginable effect on the first third of this twentieth century, in which we are now living.

My dear friends, I say this to highlight something that has no connection whatsoever with superstitious beliefs. I say it in the full knowledge of expressing an exact fact: never before have ghosts of the period directly preceding the present been so active among us as now. And if people today do not perceive these ghosts, this is not because we now live in a dark age but because, on the contrary, they are initially blinded by the light of the new dawn. It is this that makes the actions among us of the shades of the past century so fruitful for the servants of Ahriman. Today the servants of Ahriman are working in a particularly harmful way, without us being aware of them. They are trying to ahrimanically galvanize as many of these ghosts of the past century as possible, so as to bring an influence to bear on human beings today.

There is no better way of cultivating this ahrimanic trait of our time than to form popular associations and societies that promote and disseminate the erroneous ideas of the past century, which anyone with insight can see are now long superseded and outmoded. There has never been a time in which amateurs so strongly popularized the errors of a previous century. In fact, if we want to acquaint ourselves with the nature of ahrimanic deeds we can best do so wherever meetings are held based on ordinary, everyday consciousness. There are many opportunities today to discover ahrimanism in the world, for it exerts an extraordinarily strong influence. And it is Ahriman who by this means prevents people from absorbing the new element they need into their hearts and souls. This is something new that must now come into its own because it simply was not there before; must see the light of day as it does in anthroposophy.

People are content if they can in some way cover over the new, which is now coming to light in anthroposophy, with some old saying. You only need to note the pleasure people show when they can respond to something I say in a lecture by saying: 'Ah, I've read this before somewhere, in an old book.' Yet what they refer to is expressed quite differently, from a very different state of consciousness! People have so little courage for receiving what grows out of contemporary conditions that they feel relieved if they can cite something from the past to equate it with.

This shows how strongly past impulses work on people today, and how relieved they feel when past impulses work upon them. This is due to the strong influence of the nineteenth century perpetuated into the twentieth. Future observers of our present period of history, who will describe events in their spiritual context rather than merely drawing on documentation as we do today, will above all see that the beginning of the twentieth century—its first three decades in particular—stood very much in the shadows of the end of the nineteenth century, as if what was done then really consisted of the shadow deeds of human beings from that earlier period.

I would like to say something that really has no political connotation. Politics has no part in our Anthroposophical Society. I wish merely to characterize the following simple facts in regard to the tumultuous deeds—no, not deeds, but events—the tumultuous events of the second decade of the twentieth century. It has now been said so often that it has become a truism that such tumultuous events are unprecedented in history. And yet people stand within these tumultuous events as if they were uninvolved! People everywhere go about their daily lives as if these shattering events were taking place quite separately from them, as if human beings were playing no part in them. I feel like asking almost everyone I meet whether they were actually present during the second decade of the twentieth century. Or, to look at it from a slightly different point of view, how helpless people seem, how endlessly helpless: how helpless in their judgements and actions. It has never been so hard as it is at present to find ministers of state to appoint. Just think how odd what is happening really is, how helpless people are in relation to events. It's not too far-fetched to ask whether anyone is doing anything! Who is actually participating? Well I'll tell you: more than the people alive today, my dear friends, it's the people from the last third of the nineteenth century whose shadow forces are active everywhere...

1. Tracing the Threads of Karma

Lecture given at the Goetheanum on 6 July 1924

We have seen how the study of karma, encompassing human destiny, leads us from the furthest reaches of the cosmos—the starry worlds—down to the most intimate experiences of the human heart, in so far as the heart is an expression of all that we feel working upon us throughout life, of all that we undergo in earthly existence. When we try to form judgements based on a deeper understanding of karmic relationships, we find ourselves repeatedly faced with the need to examine these two realms of existence that are so far removed from each other. In fact we have to recognize that whatever else we may be studying, nature, say, or the more external aspects of human evolution and history, or cultural differences between peoples, none of these leads us so far into cosmic realms as the study of karma. More than anything else this study gives us insight into the connections between human life on earth and what occurs in the far reaches of the universe. We see this human life of ours taking its course on earth until it reaches certain limits at around the age of 70. Whatever extends beyond this we can regard, in fact, as a gift of grace. Before this point our life is subject to karmic influences, and these we will now consider.

As I have mentioned before from various points of view, however, we can reckon the length of human life on earth as being about 72 years. This number, when seen in relation to the secrets of the cosmos, is in fact a remarkable one, whose significance really only properly dawns on us when we examine what I would call the cosmic secret of human life on earth. We have already described the real nature of the stars from a spiritual perspective. When we embark on a new life on earth we return, you can say, from the world of stars to this life on earth.

And here it is striking that ancient ideas, even if our point of departure is not one based on old traditions, simply emerge of their own accord when we approach a relevant field of study with the help of modern spiritual science. We have seen how the various planets and fixed stars participate in human life and in all that penetrates and permeates it. If we examine the full scope of a human life, one that has not ended too soon but has passed through at least half of the allotted span, we can see that our descent from spiritual worlds of the cosmos to earthly existence is, ultimately, always a journey earthwards from a particular star. We can trace this direction, and it is not too vague—indeed it is precise—to say that a person has 'his star'. A certain star, a fixed star, is the spiritual home of each human being. And if we examine what we experience beyond space and time between death and a new birth, and transpose this into a spatial image, we can say that every person has his star, which is specific to what he gains and learns between death and a new birth.

He descends from the direction of a particular star, and so our hearts and minds can be informed by the idea that the human race consists, across all the continents, of those who are currently incarnated. But where are the others who are not on this earth at present? Where do we find them in the universe? Where in the wide universe must we look if we wish to turn our soul's gaze to find them, after a certain period has elapsed since they passed through the gate of death? We look in the right direction when we gaze out into the starry heavens. That is where the souls are—or at least that is the direction which will enable us to find these souls—as they pass between death and a new birth. To see the whole human race we have to look both upwards to the cosmos and downwards to earth.

Only those who are on their way there or returning again can be found in the planetary region. But when we think of the midnight hour of existence between death and a new birth we cannot do so without thinking of some star where, in a certain sense (but recalling also what I said about the nature of the stars), the human being dwells between death and a new birth.

Then, my dear friends, we shall approach the cosmos with this knowledge: out there are the stars, the cosmic signs from which the living souls of those passing between death and a new birth shimmer and gleam towards us. And then we become aware that we can also look at the starry constellations and ask ourselves how all of them are connected with human life; we can learn to look upwards in a different way, with a new, more feeling gaze, to the silvery moon, the sun's dazzling blaze, the twinkling stars at night, feeling ourselves united with all this also in human terms. This is what anthroposophy needs to achieve for human souls: they should feel themselves humanly connected with the whole cosmos. And then certain secrets of cosmic existence will also begin to dawn on us.

My dear friends, the sun rises and sets, and the stars rise and set. We can examine how the sun for example sets in the region of a certain constellation. We can trace what people nowadays call the 'apparent' course of the stars circling the earth. We can trace the course of the sun. Over 24 hours the sun circles the earth—only 'apparently' of course—and the stars also circle the earth. This is what we say, but it is not quite accurate. For if we continually and repeatedly observe the course of the stars and the sun we see at length that the latter does not rise always at the same time in relation to the stars. Each day the sun arrives just a little later at the place it was the previous day in relation to the stars. And this small difference of time by which the sun remains behind the stars gradually accumulates into one, two, then three hours, and at last a whole day. At length the time approaches when we can say that the sun is a whole day behind its original position in relation to the stars.

Now let us imagine that someone is born on 1 March in a certain year and that he lives to the age of 72. He will always celebrate his birthday on 1 March, since that is the date set by the sun. And he is also fully entitled to celebrate it then, for throughout the 72 years of his life the sun, though it also gradually falls behind the stars, continues to shine from the vicinity of the star that shone down upon his arrival on earth. But when he has lived for 72 years, a whole day has elapsed: he arrives at an age in life when the sun leaves the star into which it had just entered as he was born. When his birthday comes round he has gone beyond the first of March. The star no longer accords with the sun. The stars say that it is the second of March, while the sun still says it is the first. The person has thus lost a cosmic day, for the sun takes precisely 72 years to fall back one day behind the stars.

A human being can live on earth during this period when the sun remains in the region of his star. Then, under normal circumstances, when the sun no longer reassures a person's star about his earthly existence—when it no longer tells the star, 'He is there below, and what he has to give you I will myself give you while I temporarily hide you from view, and will do with him what you would otherwise do with him between death and a new birth'—then the star asks for the human being back again.

And here you have the processes of the heavens in direct connection with human existence on earth. We see expressed in the secrets of the heavens the human span of life. The human being can live for 72 years because the sun falls one day behind the stars during this period. Then it can no longer reassure a star which it previously reassured by standing directly in front of it, and so the star becomes free once more to engage in a person's soul-spiritual work within the cosmos.

These things can only be grasped through reverence—the profound reverence which the ancient mysteries called 'reverence for the exalted'. This reverence for exalted things repeatedly leads us to see what happens here on earth in connection with what unfolds in the sublime, majestic script of the stars. Human beings today certainly lead a narrow life compared to what still existed at the beginning of the third post-Atlantean epoch. Then people's view of the human being was not based solely on his earthly progress and circumstances but rather on what the stars of the universe say about human life.

Once we are attentive to such connections and can receive them reverently into our souls, then we will also become aware that all that happens on earth has its corresponding counterpart in worlds of spirit. The script of the stars expresses the connection between what occurs here and what—when we view things from an earthly perspective—has occurred some time previously in the world of spirit. In fact, every reflection on karma should be accompanied by deep reverence and awe before the secrets of the universe.

With this kind of profound reverence let us now approach the studies of karma which we wish to undertake in the coming days. To start with let us take this fact: a number of people are sitting here, a section of what we call the Anthroposophical Society. And while one person may be linked more strongly and another less strongly to this Anthroposophical Society, in every case it is part of some-one's destiny—and this underlying destiny is a powerful one—that a person finds his way into the Anthroposophical Society. And it is inherent in the spiritualization which the Anthroposophical Society should find since the Christmas Foundation Meeting to become increasingly aware of the spiritual and cosmic aspects underlying such a community. With this conscious awareness a person will then be able to take his true place within the Society. So you will under-stand—along with all the other responsibilities resulting from the Christmas Foundation Meeting—that we must now begin to say something, too, about the karma of the Anthroposophical Society. This is very complex, for it is a common, shared karma that arises from the karmic con-vergence of many individuals. If you take in its true and deep sense all that has been said in these lectures, and all that has also arisen from other observations made here, then, my dear friends, you will see that much of what occurs here amongst us—where a number of people are led by their karma into the Anthroposophical Society—was preceded by other occur-rences in which these people participated before they entered earthly existence, and that these were in turn the after-effect of events that occurred in previous lives on earth.

Allow yourselves to dwell for a moment on the great vistas which such an idea opens up and you will realize how this thought may gradually deepen to reveal the spiritual history underlying the Anthroposophical Society. But this cannot be done all at once. It can only enter our awareness slowly and gradually, and only then can such awareness make it possible for the actions undertaken by the Anthroposophical Society to be founded on these underlying depths which are certainly present in anthroposophists.

It is anthroposophy which keeps this Society together. In one way or another, everyone who finds his way into the Society must be seeking anthroposophy. The causes of this are the prior experiences—we won't at present look further than this—which the souls who become anthroposophists underwent before they descended to earthly existence.

At the same time, if we look out into the world with a certain insight into what really occurred then, we will find many people whom, if we examine their connection with their pre-earthly existence, we can see were destined by their pre-earthly life for the Anthroposophical Society but, due to certain circumstances, have been unable to find their way into it. There are far more of such people than we generally recognize.

But this must bring still closer to our hearts the question of the nature of predestination that leads a soul to anthroposophy.

I will start with extreme instances that are all the more instructive for showing how karmic forces work. In the Anthroposophical Society the question of karma does indeed arise more intensely for an individual than in other realms of life. I just want to point out the following. Assume for a moment that the souls who are at present incarnated in a human body mostly cannot—indeed cannot at all—have experienced in past lives anything of what leads them within the anthroposophical movement to eurythmy, to take a radical example. Eurythmy of course did not yet exist when the souls who now seek it were last incarnated.

The burning question therefore is how a soul finds its way to eurythmy through the working of karmic forces. But the same applies to all areas of life. There are souls today who seek what anthroposophy can give them. How do the pre-conditions of their karma from past lives lead them in the direction of anthroposophy?

In the first place there are some souls who are impelled towards anthroposophy with great inner intensity. Such intensity is not the same in all. Some souls are driven to anthroposophy with such inward intensity that it seems they steer straight for it, looking neither to right nor left, and find their way directly into one area or other of anthroposophical life.

There are a number of souls in whom such universal direction is inherent because, in past centuries, during their former life on earth, they felt with particular intensity that Christianity had arrived at a certain turning point. They lived at a time when Christianity primarily led people into a more or less instinctive experience. This was a time when Christianity was practised in a self-evident but also quite instinctive way, so that souls barely questioned why they were Christians. We find such souls particularly if we turn our gaze to the thirteenth, twelfth, eleventh, tenth, ninth and eighth centuries AD. There we find Christ-permeated souls who were growing and evolving towards the age of consciousness, but who had absorbed Christianity into their purely sentient soul as the age of the consciousness soul had not yet arrived. Nevertheless, in relation to more worldly matters, what the consciousness soul was to bring had already begun to dawn in them.

Thus you can say that their Christianity lived unconsciously. In many respects it was a deeply pious Christianity but it lived, in a certain sense, by avoiding the head and entering directly into organic functions. What is unconscious in one life becomes a degree more conscious in the next. And so this Christianity, which had not become fully clear about itself, became a challenge to them to ask: 'Why are we Christians?'

The outcome of this—and today I am just sketching an introduction to the theme which we will pursue further on another occasion—was that in their life between death and a new birth these souls had a certain connection once more in the worlds of spirit, especially in the first half of the nineteenth century. During this period souls gathered in the world of spirit and connected the Christianity they had experienced here on earth with the radiance and all-embracing light, the universal revelation of the world of spirit. In the first half of the nineteenth century in particular there were souls in the life between death and a new birth who endeavoured to transpose into cosmic imaginations what they had felt, as Christians, in a previous life on earth. The very thing I once described here as a great sacrament and act of worship took place in the supersensible realm. And a great number of souls gathered and were encompassed in these mutually woven, cosmic imaginations, in these mighty tableaux of a future existence, which they would seek again in altered form during their subsequent life on earth.

But interwoven with all this were also all the arduous inner conflicts—much more dire than people usually think—that had taken place between the seventh and thirteenth centuries AD. The souls of those I am referring to underwent considerable turmoil during this particular period. And they wove all that they had experienced into those mighty cosmic imaginations which, during the first half of the nineteenth century, a large number of souls were weaving together.

The cosmic imaginations woven then were shone through, on the one hand, by something I can only describe as feelings of longing and expectancy. These discarnate souls experienced these mighty imaginations, as they developed, as a concentrated feeling within them, condensed from a multiplicity of details. It was a feeling which I can describe roughly in the following way: 'In our last life on earth we felt devotion to an experience of Christ. We had a deep experience of these mysteries that tradition had preserved for Christians, relating to the sacred and solemn events in Palestine at the beginning of the Christian era. But did he really stand before us in all his glory, in his full radiance?' This question rose from their depths, and they asked: 'Wasn't it only after our death that we learned how Christ had descended from cosmic heights to the earth, as sun being? He is here no longer, but has united with the earth. Here we can only find something like a great, cosmic memory of him. We must find our way back again to the earth in order to have Christ before our souls.'

A longing for Christ accompanied these souls from then on as, with the spiritual beings of the hierarchies, they wove the mighty and sublime cosmic imaginations. This longing went with them from their pre-earthly life into their present life on earth.

This is something that spiritual vision can experience with striking intensity when it observes what took place in mankind, both incarnate and discarnate, during the nineteenth and twentieth centuries. And all kinds of things were mingled with these impressions. We must remember that the souls who now reappear shared, in their feeling for Christ, in all that took place in the struggle between those striving for Christianity and those still rooted in the ideas of ancient paganism (which was still often the case during the centuries I have referred to). In these souls, therefore, many of those influences are present which place the soul under the sway of Lucifer on the one hand and under the sway of Ahriman on the other. Ahriman and Lucifer, as we have already seen, interweave with karma just as much as the good gods.

All that was thus interwoven into the karmic effects now unfolding today must be traced in detail if we really wish to penetrate the spiritual foundations of anthroposophical endeavour. If the Christmas Foundation Meeting is to be taken seriously, the time has certainly arrived to draw aside the veil from certain things. But we must bring the proper gravity to bear on them.

Let us begin, as I said, with a radical instance; and while we do so, let all that has been said so far continue to resonate in the background.

Human souls who seek the Anthroposophical Society, and also remain in it for a time, find their way from pre-earthly into earthly existence, and pass through education and experiences here on earth. Among these souls let us take a particular instance of someone who appears as an ardent, perhaps even over-ardent member of the Anthroposophical Society, but then subsequently becomes one of its fiercest opponents. Let us observe the working of karma in an extreme case of this kind.

Someone joins the Anthroposophical Society and shows himself to be an ardent member, yet after a while he some-how manages to be not just an opponent but one who also makes derogatory remarks—basically a very strange karma.

Let's take a single instance, one soul. We look back into a

past life on earth, to a time when old memories from the pagan era still lingered on alluringly for people. It was a time when, on the one hand, people were finding their way into Christianity, which was spreading with a certain fiery warmth but which many nevertheless absorbed with a certain superficiality.

When we speak of such things we must remember that we have to begin somewhere—with a particular life on earth. Every such earthly life leads back in turn to earlier ones, so there will always be some things that remain unexplained, which we refer to simply as a given. These are of course the karmic consequences of still earlier events, but we have to begin somewhere.

In the period I just referred to, we find a certain soul—in fact we find him in a way that very closely concerned myself and other present members of this Society. We find him as a kind of would-be maker of gold, in possession of writings and manuscripts which he is hardly able to understand but interprets in his own way and then, using the instructions they contain, undertakes experiments although he has no real notion of what he is doing—for it is no simple thing to gain insight into the spiritual dimension of chemical relationships. So we see him as an experimenter, with a small library of the most diverse instructions and formulae that extend a long way back to Moorish and Arabian sources. We see him pursuing this activity in a rather out-of-the-way place, yet one visited by many inquisitive people. At last, as an effect of the practices in which he engages without any understanding, he gets a strange complaint or debility which attacks his larynx in particular, and—this being a male incarnation—his voice becomes hoarser and hoarser until it almost fades away altogether.

Now at this time Christian teachings are widespread, and are taking hold. On the one hand this man is greedy to make gold and, by so doing, to achieve all the other things that would have accompanied such success in those days. On the other hand, Christianity touches him in a way that is really full of reproaches. A kind of not altogether pure Faustian feeling arises in him, and he asks himself intensely whether he has not, perhaps, done terrible wrong. Gradually, under the influence of such thoughts, a sceptical view develops and comes to live in him that he has lost his voice as a divine punishment, a just punishment for meddling with things he ought not.

In this state of mind he sought the advice of people who have now also become connected with the Anthroposophical Society and who at the time were able to intervene in his destiny in such a way that they rescued his soul from these profound doubts. We can say that they actually saved his soul in a certain sense. But all this took place under conditions which meant that the accompanying feelings he experienced were strong but external ones. On the one hand he was overwhelmed with a sense of gratitude towards those who had rescued his inner soul life but, on the other—unclear as it all was—an appalling ahrimanic impulse became mingled with it. A strong inclination towards unrighteous magical practices was succeeded by a not wholly authentic sense of himself as entering into Christian righteousness. There was an ahrimanic aspect mingled with all this. Because it spread unclarity in his soul, his gratitude was mingled with an ahrimanic quality that transformed his thankfulness into an unworthy expression. This appeared to his soul again during the period between death and a new birth, when he arrived at the point which I described, in the first half of the nineteenth century. There he had to live through it again, and experience the deep unworthiness of what his soul had developed in that earlier life in the form of superficial, external, even cringing gratitude.

We see this picture of ahrimanized gratitude mingled with the cosmic imaginations of which I spoke. And we see the soul descend from pre-earthly life into a new earthly existence. And we see him descend with, on the one hand, all the impulses that entered into him at the time he was seeking to make gold—the materialistic corruption of a spiritual striving. At the same time we see developing in him, under the ahrimanic influence, something we can clearly perceive as a sense of shame about his improperly expressed and superficial gratitude.

These two currents live in his soul as he descends to earth, and come to expression as follows. The soul, having become a person again in earthly life, finds his way to the others who were with him at the point I described in the nineteenth century.

To begin with, a kind of memory arises in him of what he underwent in the imaginative picture of his unworthy, externalized gratitude. All this unfolds in a kind of automatic way. There awakens what lives in him and which I described as a sense of shame about his own human unworthiness. This takes hold of his soul, but since—of course due also to still earlier lives—this soul has an ahrimanized quality, he exudes something like a terrible hatred of all that he had at first espoused. This sense of shame, redirected, is transformed into wild and angry opposition, and simultaneously combined with dreadful disappointment that what lives unconsciously in him has found such little satisfaction—which he would only have found if something similar to his improper art of gold making had come about.

You see, my dear friends, here we have a radical example of how things change inwardly, of how we must seek in a former life, for example, for the connection between a sense of shame and hatred if we are to understand what has given rise to the circumstances of a present life.

If we observe such things then some understanding can be brought to bear on all that human beings bring about in the world. Great difficulties become apparent when we take the idea of karma seriously; and we should do so, for such difficulties are intrinsic to the whole nature and essence of human life. And a movement such as anthroposophy is inevitably exposed to a great deal, for only in this way can it develop the strength it needs.

I gave you this example first so that you could see how we must seek even negative things in the karmic circumstances which inform the whole destiny arising in the anthroposophical movement from previous incarnations of those united in this Society.

My dear friends, in this way we can be optimistic that a quite new understanding of the nature of the Anthroposophical Society will gradually awaken, and that we can as it were examine and gain insight into the soul of the Anthroposophical Society with all its difficulties. For here too we must not restrict ourselves to the scope of a single life on earth but must look further back to what—I cannot say reincarnates—resurfaces, and is re-experienced. And that is what I wanted to start with today.

2. The Convergence of Two Groups

Lecture given at the Goetheanum on 8 July 1924

Today I wish to include certain things in our observations that will subsequently make it easier for us to trace the karmic circumstances of the anthroposophical movement itself. This will take its point of departure from the fact that there are two groups of people within the anthroposophical movement. I have already generally described how the anthroposophical movement is composed of the individuals within it. The statement that there are two groups of people in the anthroposophical movement must initially be taken in a general way, but the aspects I wish to describe are not so easily discernible. Simple observation will not tell us that a particular member belongs to one group and another to the other. Much of what I will describe today does not lie in each person's full, daylight awareness but, like most karmic circumstances, in their instincts, in the subconscious. Such things do however certainly inform their character, temperament, ways of acting and actual deeds.

The first group to distinguish are people who feel related to Christianity in a particularly strong and heartfelt way. In these souls lives a longing to call themselves, as anthroposophists, Christians in the true sense of the word as they conceive it.

This group derives great comfort from the fact that it can be said, in the widest and fullest sense, that the anthroposophical movement is one that acknowledges and bears the Christ impulse within it. This group would suffer pangs of conscience if this were not the case.

The other group express and reveal themselves in a no less sincerely Christian way, yet they approach Christianity from a rather different angle. To begin with, they find great satisfaction in anthroposophical cosmology—the evolution of the earth from other planetary conditions and suchlike. They find satisfaction in all that anthroposophy says about the human being in general, and from this perspective they are led naturally to Christianity. But they do not, to the same degree, feel such an inward, heartfelt need to place their prime focus on Christ.

As I said, these things unfold largely subconsciously, but those who can practise soul observation can assess each individual accordingly.

Now the origins of these two groups go back to very ancient times. From reading my book *Occult Science* you will know, my dear friends, that at a certain period of Earth evolution souls as it were took leave of ongoing earthly evolution and went to dwell on other planets. Then, during a certain per-iod—Lemurian and Atlantean times—they returned to earth. And we know that the original mysteries, the oracles I described in my *Occult Science*, derived from the fact that souls descended from the various planets, from Jupiter, Saturn, Mars, etc. and also the sun, to take on human form.

Now, due to very ancient karma, many among those souls inclined to the stream which later became the Christian one. We should remember that barely a third of people on earth are practising Christians today. Thus only a certain number can be said to have developed the inclination, the impetus, to find their way into the Christian stream. The souls des-cended at different times. There were those who descended comparatively soon, during the first periods of Atlantean civilization. But there were also those who came down relatively late, and whose sojourn in pre-earthly, planetary life was therefore long. When we look back into the life of such a soul—starting from the present incarnation—we may come to a former Christian incarnation and maybe yet another Christian incarnation. Then we arrive at pre-Christian incarnations. But relatively soon we reach such a soul's earliest incarnation and must then recognize that if we pursue its life still further back than this it rises into planetary realms. Before this point such a soul was not yet present in earthly incarnation.

In the case of other souls who also found their way to Christianity things are different. We can go much further back and find many more incarnations. The other souls ultimately immersed themselves in Christianity after many pre-Christian and also Atlantean incarnations.

A more intellectual approach will regard what I have stated as extremely perplexing. One might easily be led to think that those whom contemporary civilization regards as out-standing minds are the ones who passed through many earthly incarnations. But this need not be the case at all. On the contrary, people thought to have skills and talents in the modern sense—those with the skills that enable them to grasp life fully—can certainly be the ones for whom we find comparatively fewer past incarnations.

Perhaps I may remind you here of what I presented at the Christmas Foundation Meeting as inauguration of the anthroposophical stream now informing the anthroposophical movement. I spoke of the individualities with whom the epic of Gilgamesh is connected,[1] explaining certain things about them. Tracing back the development of one of them we find that this soul had relatively few incarnations, whereas others had many more.

Now for those human souls who today find their way to anthroposophy—irrespective of whether there are other, intervening incarnations—the important one fell roughly in the third, fourth or fifth century after Christ. Sometimes it is later, even as late as the seventh or eighth century, but it is usually there, somewhere in the course of two or three centuries. Our main focus here is on the experiences such souls had at this time, which were then consolidated in a later incarnation. Today, though, I want to touch as precisely as possible on what we may call this first Christian incarnation.

The important thing about these souls is how, based on their previous capacities and experiences in former lives, they approached Christianity. You see, my dear friends, this is a very important karmic question. Later on we shall have to consider other, less primary karmic issues. But this one is a cardinal one, because if we overlook many other, less central things, people come to the Anthroposophical Society through their deepest, innermost experiences in former incarnations—such as the experiences they underwent in relation to world views, religious beliefs and suchlike. Therefore when we come to examine the karma of the Anthroposophical Society we need to focus on the experiences of these souls, their insights, world views and religious outlook.

Now, in those early centuries of Christianity it was still possible to start from traditional knowledge about the being and nature of Christ that had been present since Christianity was founded. Such knowledge referred to the fact that the one who lived as Christ in the individuality of Jesus was regarded as a sun dweller or sun being before he embarked on life on earth. One should not think that the attitude of the Christian world to these things was always as dismissive as it is today. In the first centuries of Christianity people still understood certain passages of the Gospels that clearly speak of the being called Christ as one who descended from the sun to a human body. How they conceived this specifically is less important for the moment. The point is that they held this view.

At the same time, in the epoch of which I am now speaking, the possibility of really understanding that a sun being descended to earth had diminished. In particular the souls with a large number of incarnations behind them, extending far back into Atlantean times, approached Christianity with scarcely any understanding of how one could call the Christ a sun being. The very souls who, in their ancient beliefs, had felt themselves connected with the sun oracles and who thus revered the Christ even in Atlantean times, inasmuch as they gazed up to the sun—and who were, therefore sun Christians or, as St Augustine said, 'Christians before Christianity was founded'[2]—were the ones who, due to the whole character of their spiritual life, were unable to understand that the Christ was a sun hero. They therefore preferred to hold fast to a belief which, without such interpretation or Christian cosmology, simply regarded Christ as a God from unknown realms who had united with the body of Jesus. They accepted the Gospel on this basis. They could no longer turn their gaze upwards to the cosmic world in order to understand the being of Christ precisely because they had only become acquainted with Christ in worlds beyond the earth. Because the earth mysteries, the sun oracles, had always spoken of Christ as a sun being, they could not relate to the view that this Christ, this Christ from cosmic worlds, had actually become a being of earth.

When these Christian souls later passed through the gate

of death, they found themselves in a strange situation which I will describe, though perhaps somewhat superficially, as follows. In their life after death these Christians experienced things rather as someone who knows the name of another person and has heard many things about him, but has never actually come to know him. It can then happen that his inner life fails him, that all the support which served him as long as he merely knew his name is removed, when he is suddenly expected to know the actual person. This is what happened to the souls of whom I have spoken, who in ancient times had felt themselves especially to belong to the sun oracles. In their life after death they found themselves in a situation in which they had to ask: 'Where is the Christ? We are now amongst the beings of the sun and we have not found him.' They had not really absorbed into their thoughts and feelings, which remained with them after they passed the threshold of death, the fact that he was on earth. After death, therefore, they found themselves in a state of great uncertainty about the Christ and they lived on in this uncertainty. Thus, in a succeeding incarnation, they had the tendency or inclination to join those groups of people which the religious history of Europe describes as heretical associations. But whether or not they reincarnated in the intervening period, they found themselves together again in that great gathering above the earth which I described the other morning as taking place during the first half of the nineteenth century. It was then that these souls found themselves face to face with a great supersensible sacrament and communion consisting of mighty imaginations. And in the sublime imaginations of that supersensible sacrament the sun mystery of Christ was, above all, enacted before their spiritual gaze. The aim of this was that these souls, whose Christianity had as it were come to a dead end, should, before they returned to an earthly life, be led towards the Christ in pictures at least. Although they had not entirely lost him, they had done so to the extent that he had become mingled in their souls with currents of doubt and uncertainty.

Now these souls responded in a singular way. It was not that the visions shown them led them into still greater uncertainty—it did give them a kind of reassurance in their life between death and a new birth, and a sense of redemption from certain doubts. But it also gave them a kind of memory of what they had absorbed about Christ in a form that was not yet permeated by the Mystery of Golgotha in the right way, the cosmic way. Thus there remained in their inmost being an immense warmth and devotion of feeling towards Christianity, and at the same time a subconscious dawning of those sublime imaginations. And all this was concentrated in a great longing that they might now be Christians in the true sense. Then, when they descended again, became young once more and returned to earth at the turn of the nineteenth to the twentieth centuries, they could not do otherwise—because they had absorbed the Christ in their former, early Christian incarnation in a soulful way, without cosmic understanding—than feel themselves impelled towards him. But the impressions they had received in the imaginations to which they had been drawn in their pre-earthly life remained in them only as an undefined longing. Thus it was difficult for them to find their way into the anthroposophical world view to the extent that the latter focuses first on the whole cosmic context before coming to a view of Christ.

Why did they have such difficulty? For the simple reason that they had their own very particular relationship to the question 'What is anthroposophy?' Let us ask what the reality of anthroposophy is. My dear friends, if you gaze upon all those wonderful, sublime imaginations that were revealed there as a supersensible sacrament and communion in the first half of the nineteenth century, and if you translate all these into human concepts, then you have anthroposophy.

Anthroposophy was already there in the first half of the nineteenth century for the next higher level of experience— for the world of spirit closest to the earth, from which human beings descend to the earth. It was not yet on earth but it was in that adjoining realm. And when people have a vision and perception of anthroposophy today, they see it by gazing towards the first half of the nineteenth century. That is where it can be seen, quite as a matter of course. It can even be seen already at the end of the eighteenth century.

You see, people can have the following experience. An individual was once in a peculiar situation. A friend of his posed the great riddle of human existence on earth, but this friend was rather caught up in Kant's angular thinking,[3] and thus his question was formulated in an abstract philosophical way. The individual I am speaking of, could not embrace Kant's 'angular' mode of thought. Yet this question 'How are reason and sensory nature related in the human being?' stirred up everything in his soul. And suddenly not just doors but floodgates opened, which for a moment allowed the regions of the cosmos to shine in to his soul where those mighty imaginations were unfolding. And all this, entering him not through windows or doors but in a great flood, surfaced in his soul transposed into what one might call little tableaux, and came to expression as *The Fairy Tale of the Green Snake and the Beautiful Lily*. For the individual to whom I refer was Goethe.

Miniature tableaux, small mirror images, transposed into charming form, descended in this way in Goethe's tale of *The Green Snake and the Beautiful Lily*. It is therefore not so surprising that, when the need arose to present anthroposophy in artistic images, drawing on these imaginations I have spoken of, my Mystery play *The Portal of Initiation* acquired a similar structure—though different in content—to *The Fairy Tale of the Green Snake and the Beautiful Lily*.

You see, one can gain insight into a present context by gazing back into what preceded it. Anyone with some familiarity of occult facts knows that what happens on earth is the reflection downwards of something that occurred long before in the world of spirit, though somewhat altered, inasmuch as certain spirits of obstruction and hindrance are mingled with it.

So these souls who were preparing to descend into earthly existence at the end of the nineteenth or beginning of the twentieth century brought with them a certain subconscious longing to know something, also, of cosmology and such-like—in other words to view the world in the way that anthroposophy does. But above all their hearts and minds were deeply devoted to Christ, and therefore they would have felt pangs of conscience if what they felt drawn to in pre-earthly life as the vision and outlook of anthroposophy had not been penetrated with the impulse of Christ. Such was the one group, very roughly and generally speaking of course.

The other group experienced things differently. When they emerged in their present incarnation this other group, if I can put it like this, had not yet wearied of paganism in the way that was true of the souls whom I just described. Compared to those others they had spent only a relatively short time on earth, and had passed through fewer incarnations. And in these incarnations they had been filled with those sublime impulses which one can have by nurturing, through many earth lives, a living connection with the many pagan gods, in a way that allows this connection to resonate strongly in later incarnations. Thus they had not grown weary of the ancient paganism. Even in the first centuries of Christianity the old pagan impulses had still been working strongly in them: although they did incline more or less to Christianity it gradually emerged from pagan views. At this time these souls primarily absorbed Christianity through their heart-warmed intellect—but still, nevertheless, through their intellect. They thought a great deal about Christianity. You should not imagine that this was a very scholarly type of thinking. They were often relatively simple people, in simple circumstances; but they thought a great deal.

Once again it does not matter whether a subsequent incarnation occurred in the intervening period. Such an incarnation will of course have wrought some changes, but the essential thing is that, after passing through the gate of death, these souls looked back on earth and saw Christianity as something they still needed to grow into. They had not tired of ancient paganism, and still bore within their souls a strong pagan impetus. Thus they were still waiting, as it were, for the time when they would become true Christians.

Precisely the people of whom I spoke to you a week ago, saying how they fought for Christianity and against paganism, were nevertheless among those who still in fact had a strong pagan aspect and many pagan impulses in their souls. They were really still waiting to become true Christians. These souls passed through the gates of death and arrived in the world of spirit. They passed through the life between death and a new birth and, at the period I mentioned—in the first half of the nineteenth century or a little before—they found themselves before those sublime and glorious imaginations, seeing them to be full of impetus to fire their work and deeds. They primarily received these impulses into their will. And if we now look with occult vision at all that these souls bear within them, particularly in their will, what we chiefly find in this will are the many imprints of those mighty imaginations.

But such souls who enter earthly life in this kind of state initially feel the need to re-experience here on earth, as is possible here on earth, what they underwent in their pre-earthly life as a determining factor in the work of their karma. Thus the spiritual life of the former kind of souls, the former group, unfolded in the first half of the nineteenth century in the urge and deep longing to participate in that supersensible sacrament and communion. Yet they approached it, one can say, in a vague and mystic mood, so that when they later descended to earth only dim and shadowy recollections remained in them—but these were a point of contact and understanding for anthroposophy in its now earthly form. But the second group, in contrast, rediscovered each other as it were in the after-effect of a resolve they had taken. They had not yet tired altogether of paganism but they had an expectancy that the due course of evolution would lead them to become Christians. And now it was as though they remembered a resolve they had taken during the first half of the nineteenth century: to carry down to earth all that had pervaded the mighty imaginations, and to translate this into earthly form.

When we look at the many anthroposophists who bore in them the prime inner impetus to work actively with anthroposophy, we find in them the souls of the latter group. We need to clearly distinguish between these two types.

Now, my dear friends, you may say that all this clears up some things about the karma of the Anthroposophical Society. But there may be a residual fear and anxiety about what might still be coming, things about which one might prefer to remain ignorant and not have them stirred up. Should we, you may ask, now start pondering whether we belong to the one group or the other?

I will give a very definite answer to this question, and here it is. If the Anthroposophical Society was only something that encapsulated a theoretical doctrine or a confession of belief in particular ideas about cosmology, Christology and so on, then it would not be what it essentially needs to be in accordance with its origins. In fact, anthroposophy should be something that can transform the life of a genuine anthroposophist, that can carry into a spiritual domain things that today can be experienced only in their unspiritual forms of expression.

So let me ask you: Does it have a very bad effect on a child if certain things are explained to him at a particular age? Up to a certain age children do not know whether they are French or Germans, Norwegians, Belgians or Italians. At any rate this whole way of seeing things has little significance for them, and they may even be entirely unaware of it. You won't have met three-year-old nationalists I'm sure. It is only at a certain age that people realize they are German, French or English. Surely we gradually grow into and accept such things. Do we find it unbearable to discover, at a certain age, that we are Polish, French, German, Russian or Dutch? We accommodate ourselves to these distinctions and accept them as a matter of course. But this, my dear friends, relates to the external realm of the senses. The aim of anthroposophy, in contrast, is to raise the whole of human life to a higher level. We need to learn to cope differently with things which, if we misunderstand them, might shock us in the life of the senses. And the things we need to learn to accept include gradually growing into the self-knowledge that we belong to one of these types or the other.

This will also create the foundation for properly integrating and understanding other karmic aspects of our lives. This is why, to start with, I needed to show how each person works either more passively or more actively within the anthroposophical movement in accordance with his particular type of predestination in relation to anthroposophy, to this whole area of Christology.

Of course there are intermediate types between the two groups. However, this is because a still earlier incarnation shines through what passes from a previous incarnation into the present. This is often the case with the souls of the second group in particular. Many things still shine through from their genuinely heathen incarnations, and this is why they have a definite predisposition to immediately take the Christ in the way he really should be taken, that is as a cosmic being.

But these things are apparent less in observing people's ideas than in the way they lead their lives. The two types can be recognized far more clearly by the way they handle specific situations than by their thoughts—for abstract thoughts have little significance for people. So, for instance—and of course always excluding personal dimensions—the intermediate types will often be found among those who really cannot help carrying the habits of non-anthroposophical life into the anthroposophical movement, and who really have no inclination to take the anthroposophical movement very seriously. These are people, particularly, who find fault with anthroposophists in the anthroposophical movement, and who also express much annoyance with circumstances within the anthroposophical movement itself. These intermediate types then, on the cusp between the one group and the other, are ones who find rather petty fault with individuals in the anthroposophical movement, for in such cases neither of the two impulses are very strong.

And therefore we must at all costs—even if it requires us to search our conscience and examine our character—somehow find the means, each one of us, to deepen the anthroposophical movement by approaching such issues, and by asking ourselves how our supersensible nature is related to the anthroposophical movement. By doing so a gradually stronger, more spiritualized view of the anthroposophical movement will arise. What we advocate as mere theory needs to be applied to life. When we place ourselves fully into life in accordance with such things, such theories can acquire reality. To speak much of karma, saying this or that is punished or rewarded in one way or another, does not go very deep and need not pain us at all. But when we experience such things deeply, at first hand as it were, in our own specific instance, recognizing the very particular supersensible quality underlying our present incarnation, then this touches our own being much more intimately. And it is this deepening of human nature that anthroposophy needs to introduce into life on earth, into earthly civilization.

This, my dear friends, was a kind of intermezzo and point of departure which we will continue next time.

3. Unity for Renewal: Platonists and Aristotelians

Lecture given at Arnhem on 18 July 1924

Because I arrived late yesterday I was unable to speak to you, as I wished, about what has been happening in the Anthroposophical Society since the Christmas Foundation Meeting at the Goetheanum. As the aim and purpose of that Christmas conference will by now be largely familiar to friends through the newsletter, I propose to speak only about the aspects of prime importance, and then continue with the studies which have a more inward connection with the significance of the Christmas Foundation Meeting for the Anthroposophical Society.

The Christmas Foundation Meeting was intended to be a fundamental renewal, a new foundation of the Anthroposophical Society. Up to the Christmas Foundation Meeting I was always able to make a distinction between the anthroposophical movement and the Anthroposophical Society. The latter was intended to be, as it were, the earthly projection of something that exists in worlds of spirit, in a particular stream of the life of spirit. What was taught here on earth and communicated as anthroposophical wisdom was intended to reflect what flows in worlds of spirit, in our times, in harmony with humanity's current phase of evolution. At the same time the Anthroposophical Society was also a kind of organ that as it were administrates the flow of anthroposophical teachings through the anthroposophical movement.

As time went on this did not turn out to be something that can properly connect with an authentic, true cultivation of anthroposophy. Thus it became necessary for me—for until then I had taught anthroposophy without having any official link with the Anthroposophical Society—to assume leadership of the Anthroposophical Society as such, in collaboration with the Dornach executive council. As a result, the anthroposophical movement and the Anthroposophical Society have become one. Since the Christmas Foundation Meeting in Dornach the very opposite now holds true: no distinction should any longer be made between the anthroposophical movement and the Anthroposophical Society, for they should now be one and the same thing. And those who stand beside me as the Goetheanum executive council should be regarded as a kind of esoteric executive. Thus what occurs through the vehicle of this executive can be described as anthroposophy in action, whereas formerly it existed only to administrate and oversee the teachings of anthroposophy.

At the same time, however, this also means that the whole Anthroposophical Society must gradually be placed on a new footing—one which makes it possible for esotericism to stream directly through the Society. In future, the true being of the Anthroposophical Society will consist in the corresponding response and attitude of those who wish to be anthroposophists. In consequence we will have to distinguish between the General Anthroposophical Society, which in future will be an entirely open and public organization—so that, as was announced at Christmas, lecture courses will be open to all, subject to the provisos which embody conditions of a spiritual and ideal nature—and the School now founded within this General Anthroposophical Society, which will eventually extend to three classes. So far we have only been able to launch the First Class. Those who wish to join this School will be obliged to assume responsibilities over and above those of ordinary or general members of the Anthroposophical Society. Those who are interested in anthroposophy, and engage with its teachings, can join the Anthroposophical Society; and by doing so they enter into no obligations apart from those which every decent person will gladly adopt on ethical grounds. Those who wish to become members of the School, on the other hand, will be required to represent the anthroposophical movement in their lives, and act in harmony with the esoteric executive at the Goetheanum. This means, therefore, that anyone who wishes to join the School must also endeavour to embody and represent anthroposophy in the world through his individual utterances and actions. In turn, this naturally means that if the School's leadership considers that someone is not representing the anthroposophical movement it reserves the right to state that the person concerned can no longer be a member of the School. You should not think that this implies a curtailing of human freedom. Instead there is a kind of free contractual relationship between the members of the School and its directors; for the latter must also be free to say what they wish to whomever it must be said. Therefore the leadership must also be able to highlight to anyone with whom it does not feel able to speak the fact that it cannot do so.

The fruitful development of anthroposophical concerns will depend on the whole way in which we view the esoteric aspect that from now on penetrates the anthroposophical movement. Care will be taken to ensure that the Anthroposophical Society is kept free from bureaucratic and external administrative measures, and that everything is based on a solely human element to be cultivated within the Society.

Certainly, the executive council will have an administrative role in many matters, but this will not be the core of its work. The essential thing will be that the executive council at the Goetheanum will act out of its own initiative. And what it undertakes, and has already started to undertake in all sorts of areas, will form the content of the Anthroposophical Society.

By this means a great many harmful tendencies that have arisen in the Society during recent years will be eradicated. These have caused difficulties for many members since all sorts of bodies were created—out of supposed goodwill—which did not in fact prove equal to what they claimed to be, and have actually side-tracked the anthroposophical movement. From now on the anthroposophical movement will, in a human sense, be the stream flowing through the Anthroposophical Society.

The more we realize this the more the anthroposophical movement will thrive. Let me say this: the impulse which prevailed among those who gathered at the Goetheanum at Christmas has made it possible to introduce a quite different tone into the anthroposophical movement. And to my deep satisfaction I have met a heartfelt response to this new tone in the different places I have so far been able to visit. What was undertaken at Christmas was, one has to say, fraught with risk in a certain sense. Because the leadership of the Anthroposophical Society was now directly merged with representation of spiritual wisdom and teachings, the powers in the world of spirit who lead the anthroposophical movement might have withdrawn their guiding hands. I can now say that this did not happen, but on the contrary, these spiritual powers are now responding with ever more grace and beneficence to what streams through the anthroposophical movement. In a certain sense a pledge has been made to the world of spirit. This pledge will be fulfilled unswervingly, and in future we will ensure that things occur in the way that has been promised to the world of spirit. Thus the executive council has taken on a responsibility not only to the anthroposophical movement but also the Anthroposophical Society.

I have spoken these few preliminary words only in order to lead on to something that can now be said, and whose nature is such that it can become part of the content of the anthroposophical movement. I want to speak about something that relates to the karma of the Anthroposophical Society itself.

If we observe how the Anthroposophical Society exists in the world as the embodiment of the anthroposophical movement, we can see a number of human beings coming together within this Anthroposophical Society. A discerning person will realize that there are also other people in the world—one finds them everywhere—whose karma predisposes them to approach the Anthroposophical Society. But initially they encounter hindrances, and do not immediately and fully find their way into it—though eventually they will certainly do so, either in this or the next incarnation. But we must bear the following in mind: that those people whose karma leads them to the anthroposophical movement are predestined to find it.

Now everything that occurs here in the physical world is foreshadowed in worlds of spirit. Nothing happens in the physical world that has not first been spiritually prepared in the spiritual world. And the significant thing is this: the coming together of a number of people in the Anthroposophical Society in the twentieth century was spiritually prepared during the first half of the nineteenth century, when the large number of souls now in incarnation and coming together in this movement were united in realms of spirit before descending into the physical world. In worlds of spirit at that time a kind of sacrament was enacted by a number of souls working together—a sacrament or communion which provided a preparatory impetus for those longings that have surfaced in souls who now, in their present incarnation, stream together into the Anthroposophical Society. And someone who has a gift for recognizing such souls within their bodies will indeed acknowledge them as having worked together with him in the first half of the nineteenth century, when, in the world of spirit, mighty cosmic imaginations were invoked of what I might call the new Christianity. Then, as in their bodies now, souls were united in order to draw mighty pictures of cosmic significance from what I will call cosmic substance and forces, as a prelude to what is to be fulfilled here on earth as anthroposophical teaching and practice. By far the majority of anthroposophists who now gather together would, if they perceived this, be able to say that they know one another and that they were formerly together in worlds of spirit, experiencing mighty, cosmic imaginations in a supersensible rite.

All these souls gathered together in the first half of the nineteenth century to prepare for what was to become the anthroposophical movement on earth. Basically this was all a preparation for what I have often called the Michael stream, which arose in the last third of the nineteenth century as the most incisive spiritual influx in modern humanity's phase of evolution. The Michael stream prepares the way for Michael's work in heaven and on earth: this was the task of the souls who gathered together in worlds of spirit.

However, these souls were in turn drawn together by experiences they had undergone through long, long ages— through centuries and even millennia. And among them we can distinguish two main groups. The one group experienced Christianity in the form in which it had spread through southern Europe, and also to some extent central Europe, during the first centuries of the Christian era. These adherents of Christianity saw Christ as the great, divine messenger who had descended to earth from the sun in order to continue working among human beings. With greater or less understanding, the first Christians of the earliest centuries after Christ regarded him as the 'mighty Sun God'.

But during these first Christian centuries, the faculty of instinctive clairvoyance once possessed by human beings was fading. People could no longer see in the sun the great spiritual kingdom at whose centre the Christ had once dwelt. Ancient clairvoyant perception of the descent of Christ to earth was superseded by mere tradition—a tradition that he had descended to earth from the sun and united with the physical body of Jesus of Nazareth. Most Christians now retained little more than the idea that a being—Christ Jesus—had once dwelt in Palestine. His true nature— whether he was a God, or God and man simultaneously, or something similar—now came to be the subject of controversy in the Church councils. Increasingly the masses knew nothing more than they were told in decrees issued by Rome.

Among the throng of Christians, however, lived individuals who were increasingly regarded as heretics. They preserved a living memory and tradition of the Christ as a being who had once descended to our physical and sensory earth and was, as a sun being, quite alien to it. Until the seventh and eighth centuries AD these individuals increasingly faced a situation in which, as they saw it, Christianity in its later form no longer understood Christ! In fact one can say that these 'heretics' became weary of Christianity. So there were souls who, up to the seventh and eighth centuries, passed through the gate of death with a sense of weariness about Christianity. Whether or not these souls reincarnated in the intervening period, the incarnation decisive for them was the one they underwent in the early Christian centuries. Then, from the seventh and eighth centuries onwards, they were preparing themselves in worlds of spirit for that great, mighty activity I spoke of when I referred to a kind of supersensible sacrament occurring in the first half of the nineteenth century. These souls participated in this great rite or sacrament, and are the first group of souls who have now found their way into the Anthroposophical Society.

The other group of souls had their last important incarnation in the most recent, not the earliest, Christian centuries. These were souls who, in pre-Christian, pagan times, were still able to gaze into worlds of spirit with clairvoyant vision. In these ancient mysteries they had learned that the Christ would one day descend to earth. They themselves did not live on earth during the early centuries of Christianity but remained in supersensible worlds, only descending to significant incarnations again after the seventh century. One can say that these souls, who witnessed the entry of Christ into earthly culture and civilization from a supersensible vantage point, were ones who thirsted for Christianity. At the same time they were resolute in a desire to work actively to bring a truly cosmic, spiritual form of Christianity into the world.

This second group united with the other souls to create that supersensible rite and sacrament which took place in the first half of the nineteenth century. This was a great, cosmic and spiritual festival lasting for many decades as a spiritual event in the world directly bordering on the physical realm. Souls, either weary of or thirsting for Christianity, first worked together in the supersensible world to prepare for their next incarnation on earth, before subsequently descending to it. They incarnated towards the end of the nineteenth century, and brought with them a readiness to find their way into the Anthroposophical Society.

All this was prepared through centuries. Here on earth, Christianity had come to regard the Gospels as though they spoke only of a being—Jesus of Nazareth—who proclaimed the Christ as descending from some kind of abstract heights. People no longer had any sense that the world of stars is an expression of spiritual realities and intimately connected with the world of spirit. Therefore they were also unable to understand that Christ, as a divine sun hero, descended into Jesus to share in human destiny. The facts of greatest significance are the very ones which escape the attention of ordinary academic historians. Above all, there is no understanding of those who are called 'heretics'. Moreover, most of the souls who descended to earth as the twentieth century approached—both those weary of Christianity and those who longed for it—largely fail to recognize themselves.

By the seventh and eighth centuries the traditions kept alive by these heretics who had grown weary of Christianity had gradually faded. Their knowledge was preserved and cultivated in small circles only, up until the middle of the medieval period. These small groups consisted of teachers whom one may call divinely gifted, who still cultivated something of this ancient knowledge of spiritual Christianity, of Christianity imbued by the cosmos. They also included some who received these teachings from ancient times and in whom a kind of enlightening inspiration was kindled. They were thus able to experience a reflection—either stronger or weaker—of what, in the first Christian centuries, people had been able to behold under the influence of a mighty inspiration, of the descent of the Sun God into the Mystery of Golgotha.

And so there were two main streams present. One, as we saw, arises directly from the heretical movements of the first Christian centuries. These souls were still fired by what lived in the Platonism of ancient Greece—to the extent that when their inner vision opened as a result of ancient teachings they were able, under the influence of a genuine if faint inspiration, to perceive the descent of Christ to the earth and his work there. This was the Platonic stream.

A different destiny awaited the other stream. These were primarily souls who had their last important incarnation in the pre-Christian era, and who had at that time glimpsed Christianity as something for the future. The task of this stream was to prepare the human intellect for the epoch which began in the first half of the fifteenth century. This was to be the era when the consciousness soul arose, and the human intellect developed. This epoch was prepared by the Aristotelians as opposed to the Platonists—but as harmonious counterweight to the latter. And those who propounded Aristotelian teachings until well into the twelfth century were souls who had passed through their last decisive incarnation in ancient pagan times, especially in ancient Greece. And then—in the middle of the medieval period, during the twelfth and thirteenth centuries—there occurred that great and wonderful encounter between Platonists and the Aristotelians, among whom were the leaders of those who, as the two groups of souls I have described, nurtured the anthroposophical movement.

By the twelfth century, as though through inner necessity, a certain school had arisen in which the afterglow of ancient Platonic vision was kindled once more. This was the great, illustrious school of Chartres, in which there worked great teachers who still had a connection with the mysteries of early Christianity, and in whose hearts and souls this knowledge awoke a vision of the spiritual foundations of Christianity. In this school of Chartres in France, which flourished particularly at the end of the eleventh and beginning of the twelfth century, where the magnificent cathedral stands with its profusion of wonderful detail, a knowledge was assembled and concentrated which previously had been widely dispersed in small groups. One of those connected with the school was Peter of Compostella, whose inspired understanding was able to bring ancient, spiritual Christianity to life once again in his own heart and soul. Alongside him there was a whole succession of wonderful teachers in Chartres. Truly remarkable voices spoke of Christianity during this twelfth century, for example Bernard of Chartres, Bernard Sylvestris, John of Salisbury, but above all the great Alanus ab Insulis. These were mighty teachers indeed. When they spoke in the school of Chartres it was as if Plato himself, interpreting Christianity, were working in person among them. They taught Christianity's spiritual content and substance. The writings that have come down from them may seem full of abstractions to those who read them today, but that is due merely to the abstract mode of thought of modern souls. The texts written by these great individuals describe the world of spirit as fully penetrated by the Christ impetus. And, my dear friends, I now wish to describe to you something of what Bernard of Chartres and Alanus ab Insulis in particular taught their initiated pupils. Paradoxical as it will seem to the modern mind, the pupils of the Chartres school experienced such things in those days.

They were taught that Christianity would be renewed, that its spiritual content and essence would once again be understood once Kali Yuga, the age of darkness, had come to an end at the breaking of a new dawn. This occurred in the year 1899 with a great and mighty change for humanity at the end of Kali Yuga: the huge impetus invoked through the new intervention of Michael two decades before. This was already prophetically foreseen in the school of Chartres in the twelfth century, particularly by Bernard Sylvestris and Alanus ab Insulis. But these men did not teach in the Aristotelian way, through the intellect. Instead they gave their teachings entirely in the form of unfolding mighty, imaginative pictures, which conveyed a tangible sense of Christianity's spiritual content. But there were also certain prophetic teachings, and I now wish to give you a brief extract as it were of one such teaching.

Alanus ab Insulis spoke to a small group of his initiated pupils as follows: 'As we contemplate the universe today, we still regard the earth as the centre, judging everything from this central point. If this terrestrial perspective, which enables us to form our pictures and imaginations, were the only one to develop and bear fruit in the following centuries, humanity would be unable to progress. We must come to an understanding with the Aristotelians, who introduce to humanity an intellect which must then be spiritualized so that in the twentieth century it may shine forth among human beings in a new, spiritual form. In regarding the earth as the centre of the cosmos nowadays, we speak of the planets encircling the earth, and of the whole heaven of stars before our physical eyes as if they likewise revolved around the earth. But one will come who will say, "Let us place the sun at the spatial centre of the universe"! As a result, though, the picture of the world will grow arid. People will then only calculate the orbits of the planets and merely specify the positions of the heavenly bodies, describing them as gases or burning, luminous physical entities. They will know the starry heavens only in terms of mathematical and mechanical laws. Yet this arid image of the universe that is to become widespread in future has one benefit—impoverished though it is. At present we view the universe from the earth at its centre, but the one who will come will view it from the sun as central point. He will be like someone who merely points out the "direction"—leading towards a path of majestic splendour, informed by the most wonderful events and peopled by glorious beings. But he will point out this direction in abstract terms only.' (Thus he heralded the Copernican world view, in its arid and abstract quality.) This is the direction we must go in, said Alanus ab Insulis, for all that we perceive through our imaginations must be dispensed with. It must pass away and the image people now have of the world must become altogether abstract, scarcely more than a pointer along a path strewn with wonderful memorials. For then, in the world of spirit, there will be one who will have nothing other than this direction to work with, by means of which, hand-in-hand with intellectualism, he will be able to found the new spirituality. He will be unable to use anything other than this waymarker. And this will be St Michael! The ground must be cleared for him. He must sow the path with new seed. And to that end linear, mathematical thinking must predominate.

Something like a magic shiver passed through the school of

Chartres as Alanus ab Insulis gave these teachings to just a few of his pupils. It was as if the surrounding etheric world was set astir by the surging waves of this mighty, Michaelic teaching.

And so there spread across western Europe, as far as southern Italy, what gave this world its spiritual atmosphere. And there were some who could grasp this, in whose souls something rose up like a mighty inspiration and who were then able to gaze into the world of spirit.

But in the world's evolution those who are initiated into the great secrets of existence, as was true to a certain degree of Alanus ab Insulis and Bernard Sylvestris, know that there are always limitations to what one can do! A person such as Alanus ab Insulis knew that he, and all other Platonists, must go through the gate of death and can initially live only in the world of spirit. From there, as he knew, they must gaze down and leave the physical world to others—who develop the intellect in an Aristotelian way. It was time for the intellect to be cultivated. At an advanced age, Alanus ab Insulis took Cistercian orders. And these orders embodied many of the same teachings. Yet those among them who had the deepest insights knew that they could, from then on, work only from the world of spirit, and must leave the field to the Aristotelians.

The Aristotelians mainly joined the ranks of the Dominicans, therefore assuming in the thirteenth century a dominant role in European culture. But something remained from these other minds in particular—from Peter of Compostella, Alanus ab Insulis, Bernard of Chartres, John Salisbury and the poet from the school of Chartres who composed an important work on the seven liberal arts. Something remained and exerted a significant effect on European cul-

ture. What took place in the school of Chartres was so incisive that, for example, it percolated down to the University of
Orleans where, in the second half of the twelfth century much
of it resurfaced in a more academic form, preserving something of what had previously flowed to the pupils of Chartres
in mighty imaginations, in fluid silver one might say, from the
mouths of Bernard Sylvestris and Alanus ab Insulis. The
spiritual atmosphere, we can say, was so imbued with this
quality that such things as the following occurred. On one
occasion an Italian returning from his post as Spanish
ambassador, and hastening homewards, heard news in
Florence of the overthrow of the Guelph dynasty; and this,
compounded by slight sunstroke, led to his etheric body
loosening and absorbing what remained of the etheric currents reverberating from Chartres. And what wafted etherically to him in this way gave rise in him to a kind of intuition,
similar to that present in many during the first Christian
centuries. He first saw the earthly world spreading before
him, as it surrounds us, but now not under the sway of what
were later termed natural laws but subject to the dominion of
the great handmaiden of the divine Demiurgos, Natura
herself, who took the place of Proserpine in the first Christian
centuries. In those days abstract laws of nature did not exist
as such. Initiates perceived what worked through nature as
living beings, as a universal, divine power. The Greek mysteries saw Proserpine or Persephone—who divides her time
between the upper worlds and the underworld—as the power
that rules nature. Her successor in the first Christian centuries was the goddess Natura.

After this individual had thus gazed upon the living,
weaving activity of the goddess Natura as a result of sunstroke and the wafting towards him of what the school of

Chartres cultivated, and then continued to allow this intuition to work upon him, he beheld a vision of the workings of the elements, of earth, water, air and fire, as this was perceived in the ancient mysteries. He saw the mighty interweaving of the elements. Then he saw the secrets of the human soul, and those seven powers who were known to be the great, heavenly teachers of the human race. These things were known in the first Christian centuries. In those days abstract doctrines as we have today, conveyed through concepts and ideas, had no place. In these first Christian centuries people spoke of the goddesses Dialecta, Rhetorica, Grammatica, Arithmetica, Geometria, Astrologia or Astronomia, and Musica, who imparted wisdom from worlds of spirit. These seven were not conceived in the abstract as later. People perceived them, rather, as though seeing them—not physically, but soulfully—and took instruction from these heavenly spirits. Later on they no longer appeared to people in the solitude of vision as the living goddesses Dialecta, Rhetorica and so forth, but in abstract and theoretical doctrines.

The individual of whom I am now speaking allowed all this to work upon him, and was then initiated into the planetary world which simultaneously reveals the secrets of the human soul. And, after passing through the great cosmic ocean, he was led through the world of the stars by Ovid who had passed through the gate of death and had become the guide of souls in the world of spirit. This individual, called Brunetto Latini, became the teacher of Dante. And what Dante learned from Brunetto Latini he subsequently composed in poetic form as the Divine Comedy. In other words, the Divine Comedy is a last reflection of what lived on here and there as Platonic wisdom, and which was still taught—

for example by Sylvestris—in the school of Chartres in the twelfth century, by those who received the impulse from ancient teachings, and whose souls opened to the secrets of Christianity in remarkable inspirations which they were then able to convey to their pupils in words.

What Alanus ab Insulis introduced to the Cistercian orders passed to the Dominicans, who primarily cultivated an Aristotelian type of intellect. But there was a transition period. In the twelfth century the school of Chartres flourished, and in the thirteenth, in the Dominican order, Scholasticism's great influx began, drawing on the Aristotelian tradition. Those great teachers of the school of Chartres who had ascended into the world of spirit through the gate of death were for a while in communion there with the Dominican souls who were descending to birth, and who subsequently founded the new Aristotelianism. Thus we must be aware of this intervening period during which, as though in a great, heavenly council of souls, the last great teachers of Chartres conferred after passing through the gate of death with those who were to establish Aristotelianism as Dominicans, before the latter descended to birth. There, in the world of spirit, a great 'heavenly contract' was concluded. Those led by Alanus ab Insulis, who had entered the spiritual world, told the descending Aristotelians: 'It is no longer our time on earth, and we must, for now, work from worlds of spirit instead. We cannot incarnate on earth in the coming time. It is now your task to cultivate the intellect in the dawning age of the consciousness soul.'

Then the great Scholastics descended and carried out what they had agreed with the last great Platonists from the school of Chartres. Many significant things occurred at that time. For instance, one of the earliest to descend received a message from another, who remained longer than he had with Alanus ab Insulis in the world of spirit, or rather with the spiritual individuality who had formerly been Alanus. The soul who descended later to birth brought this message; that is, he worked closely with the older one, thus beginning on earth a period of preparation for the intellectual age that had already started in the Dominican order. The same soul who had remained somewhat longer with Alanus ab Insulis in the world of spirit first took Cistercian orders, and only later changed to become a Dominican. Thus on earth were now working those who had originally been influenced by all that Aristotle developed, while above the Platonists from the school of Chartres kept watch as it were—but in living connection with the Aristotelians working on earth. The spiritual world and the physical world went hand in hand. Through the thirteenth, fourteenth and fifteenth centuries, it was as if the Aristotelians and Platonists reached out their hands to one another. And then of course many of those who had descended to introduce Aristotelianism in Europe returned to the others in the spiritual world again.

But in the further course of developments, both those who had been leaders in the School of Chartres and those who had occupied leading positions in the Dominican order, assumed leadership of the souls who were preparing the future anthroposophical stream in that mighty, supersensible sacrament in the first half of the nineteenth century, which unfolded in the great imaginations I have spoken of. Initially there descended those who had, more or less, worked as Aristotelians; for under the sway of intellectualism the time had not yet arrived for a new, more spiritual age. But there was an irreversible concord and agreement, whose effects continue. And flowing from this agreement the anthroposophical movement must give rise to something that has to find its completion before the century ends. For a destiny hovers over the Anthroposophical Society, such that many of those who are now members of the Anthroposophical Society must descend again to earth by the end of the twentieth century—but now united with those who themselves were either leaders in the Chartres School or were pupils there. Before the end of the twentieth century, if civilization is not to succumb entirely to decadence, the Chartres Platonists and the later Aristotelians must work together.

In future the Anthroposophical Society will need to become fully conscious of this fact, and understand something of its karma. The womb of humanity's spiritual evolution conceals much which cannot yet come to the surface today. Nowadays many things still appear in a very superficial guise. But if we can recognize the symptoms and inner significance of what manifests outwardly, then the veil can be drawn back from much that lives spiritually through the centuries. Let me try to touch on some of these symptoms— for why should we not do so, now that the Anthroposophical Society is to be penetrated with an esoteric impulse? I would like to touch on a few things to show you how, by observing what surrounds us, we can penetrate below the surface to find various interconnections.

I myself, in preparation for the anthroposophical movement, underwent a particular path of destiny which is connected in a strange way with the Cistercian order, which is itself connected with Alanus ab Insulis. For those who thrive on making up legends, let me say that I myself, in my own individuality, have nothing to do with Alanus ab Insulis. I really want to avoid the esoteric insights I offer being used as the stuff of legends. These things must be presented strictly from an esoteric perspective. In a curious way, then, my own destiny has allowed me to penetrate external events to what one can learn from a spiritual context such as this. Some of you may have read my *Autobiography* (originally published in the 'Goetheanum' journal). There I related the fact that in my youth, rather than attending a *Gymnasium* [equivalent to a Grammar school] I went to a *Realschule* [equivalent to a secondary modern] and only later acquired the more intellectual learning taught in a *Gymnasium*. I have to see this as strangely ordained by my karma. In the town where I grew up the *Gymnasium* and *Realschule* were just a few steps away from each other, and if things had been just a hair's breadth different I would have gone to the *Gymnasium*. But if I had attended the *Gymnasium* at the time, in that town, I would without doubt have become a priest of the Cistercian order, for this was a *Gymnasium* where only Cistercians taught. I actually felt strongly drawn to all these priests, many of whom were also extraordinarily scholarly people. I read much of what they wrote, and it went deep into me. I loved these priests. And really I only as it were sailed past the Cistercian order because I did not attend the *Gymnasium*. Karma led me elsewhere—but I could not get the Cistercian order out of my mind. I described this also in my *Autobiography*. I was always sociable by nature, and I relate there that I associated with almost every theologian in the city at the house of Marie Eugenie delle Grazie, and these were almost all Cistercian priests. So in a way a perspective opened up for me which might have led me back. For me personally these things felt very close: my gaze was led back through the Cistercian stream, through the life of the spirit, to the School of Chartres. For Alanus ab Insulis was a Cistercian. And strange to say, when I later came to write my first Mystery

play, *The Portal of Initiation*, I found myself with no other
option, based on aesthetic necessity, than to have the women
dressed in a costume consisting of a long tunic and a stole.
Imagine such dress, a yellow and white tunic, then the black
stole and black sash—and there you have the habit of the
Cistercian order. At the time I was thinking only of aes-
thetics, but in fact this costume very much resembled that of
the Cistercians. So here you have a hint of the way in which a
whole context comes into focus for someone who can trace
the inner, spiritual significance of external symptoms.

At Christmas we began increasingly to draw back the veil
on these inner connections. They must surface and see the
light of day, for humanity is waiting for insight into inner
dimensions, having experienced nothing but externalities for
many centuries now—so that civilization is, consequently, in
a dire situation. The insights we need to penetrate must
include how the School of Chartres worked on the one hand:
how the initiates of this School passed through the gate of
death and met the souls who later wore the habit of the
Dominican order, thus spreading intellectual Aristotelianism
and most powerfully preparing the age of the consciousness
soul. Here, working on in the Anthroposophical Society, one
can say, we have Aristotelianism, but now spiritualized, and
seeking further spiritualization. Then, on the other hand,
there will come at the end of the twentieth century the
souls—many of whom are already here—who unite with
those who were once teachers in the School of Chartres. The
anthroposophical movement aims to unite both of these.
Aristotelianism holds sway in the souls of those who, in
ancient heathen times, primarily looked expectantly towards
Christianity and yearned for it, until they could propound it
intellectually as Dominicans. And these souls will be united

with those who were able to experience Christianity in physical embodiment, and whose most important leaders gathered at the School of Chartres. These latter have not so far
incarnated, although, in my own encounter with the Cistercian order, I frequently experienced the epitome, as it
were, of those who were in the School of Chartres. In the
Cistercian order one can encounter individuals who, while
they are not a reincarnation of a pupil of Chartres, have had
moments in life when, for hours or even days, they were
permeated by an individuality from the Chartres School. I
call this 'incorporation' rather than incarnation. And such
times or moments have given rise to wonderful writings, so
that we can ask who has written them. The author is not the
priest in the Cistercian order at the time, in his pale yellow
habit with black stole and sash, but rather the individuality
who, for days or weeks, has occupied the soul of a Cistercian
brother. Something of such texts has worked on in essays or
writings of which little is known in literature. I myself had a
remarkable conversation, which I also relate in my *Autobiography*, with a member of the Cistercian order—an
extremely scholarly man. We were leaving a gathering
together and discussing the problem of Christ. I explained
my thoughts on this, which were fundamentally the same as
those I always present. As I spoke he grew a little agitated,
saying: 'We may be able to conceive such things, but let us
not allow ourselves to think them.' He said that or something
similar about other problems of Christology. But then—I can
still recall this moment very vividly—we halted where the
Schottenring and Burgring meet in Vienna, with the Hofburg
on one side and the Hotel de France and the Votiv Kirche on
the other, and he said to me: 'Please come with me. I will give
you a book from my library: it contains something curious

which relates to what you were just saying.' I went with him and he gave me a book about the Druze. From the whole connection between our conversation and what I found in this book I realized that the spirit of this scholarly man had in a most remarkable way been lifted out of him when I began speaking of repeated earthly lives in connection with Christology; and that when he had come back to himself he had merely remembered that he had a book about the Druze which mentioned reincarnation. He had only this one book which referred to such a thing. He was so erudite, and a councillor at Vienna University, that people used to say of him: 'N.N. knows the whole world, and three villages besides.' He was extraordinarily erudite, but in his physical existence all he knew was that he had a book about the Druze which mentioned reincarnation. This illustrates the difference between what people know in their subconscious and what streams through human souls as world of spirit. And then I was giving a lecture in Vienna once, which this same person attended. And after the lecture he made a remark which could only be interpreted as complete understanding, at that moment, of contemporary human beings and their connection with their former incarnations. What he said about the connection between two earthly lives was correct, not false. But he understood nothing—he only said it.

I just wanted to touch here on how spiritual movements affect the present. But what today just peeps in as it were through little windows must in future grow into a unity through the connection formed between the leaders of the School of Chartres and the leaders of the Scholastics. Then spiritual renewal, which also leads intellectualism into the spiritual domain, will arise with the end of the twentieth century. To make sure this happens, the people of the twentieth century must not throw away their opportunities. Yet since everything depends on free will, whether this happens or not—in other words, whether the two allied parties can descend to respiritualize culture in the twentieth century—depends on whether the Anthroposophical Society knows how to nurture anthroposophy in the right, devoted way.

This is what I wished to say today: how the anthroposophical stream is connected with the deep secret of the age which began with the appearance of Christ at the Mystery of Golgotha, and developed further in the way I have now described. We will pursue this further in the next lecture.

4. Let Michael Think in Us

Lecture given at Arnhem on 19 July 1924

Yesterday I spoke to those of you present about the karma of the Anthroposophical Society. Today I want to speak of various related things, but will do so in a way which stands on its own.

Everything we need to undertake at the present stage of humanity's development to prepare spiritual events in the near and more distant future is connected with what I have often referred to as the Michael event. Today I would like to discuss some aspects of this in its connection with the anthroposophical movement.

When speaking of something like the Michael event, we need to start from the idea that the world is as it were structured in 'stages'. If we only observe world evolution with the powers possible to us today in earthly life between birth and death we will see how humanity has evolved, how ancient peoples developed from still more ancient ones, and how gradually oriental culture—Indian, Chinese, Arabic, Chaldean and Egyptian peoples—gave rise to Greek and Roman civilization. Subsequently, the medieval period developed from Greek and Roman culture, and finally our own modern times—with all its confusion but also all its great technical achievements—has arisen. Yet both 'below', as I would like to put it, and 'above' this surface of reality that we can observe in human evolution we can see developments which do not belong to human beings but which spiritual beings undergo, although these beings are in a certain way also related to humanity's evolution.

The realm of the Angeloi, or angels in Christian terminology, is directly connected with the development of each
individual person. These are the beings who guide each
human being, to the extent that he needs such guidance,
from one earthly life to the next. They protect a human being
in whatever way he needs. Thus, even if invisible to earthly
eyes, they are directly connected with human evolution.

In the realm immediately adjoining that of the Angeloi we
find the beings whom we can call the Archangeloi or archangels. These archangels have to do with much that also
plays a role in human evolution—not with individual people
now, but with groups of people. Thus, as I have often said in
anthroposophical lectures, the evolution of whole groups of
peoples and nations is governed by archangel beings. However it is also true that certain epochs of Earth evolution draw
primary impetus from, and are determined by very particular
archangels. For instance in the three centuries preceding the
last third of the nineteenth century, that is in the nineteenth,
eighteenth, seventeenth and during part of the sixteenth
century, we must imagine the civilized world largely governed by the archangel being whom the Christians who can
speak of such things call Gabriel. In other words, this period
was the age of Gabriel.

This age of Gabriel has great significance for all latterday
human evolution. After the Mystery of Golgotha, people
were able to experience the fact that a high sun being, the
Christ, descended from the sun to earth at the Mystery of
Golgotha, and took upon himself a body in the body of Jesus
and united himself with the earth's destiny. But though the
Christ being remained united with the earth, the Christ
impulse—throughout the sequence of dominion of the
archangels from the Mystery of Golgotha to the age of

Gabriel—was not yet able to take root in humanity's inner physical and etheric forces. This only became possible under Gabriel's dominion, which began around three centuries before the last third of the nineteenth century. Only since that time, therefore, has humanity been able—although this has not yet happened—to be inwardly permeated by the Christ impetus through forces of heredity. Gabriel's role in humanity is to govern all that relates to physical heredity. He is, in fact, the supersensible spirit connected with the sequence of generations and thus, I would like to say, the great, all-embracing guardian spirit of mothers who bring children into the world. Gabriel is connected with births and human embryological development. The forces of Gabriel lie in everything which spiritually underlies physical reproduction. It is therefore really only since this latest age of Gabriel that humanity's physical reproduction has become connected with the Christ impulse.

Then, from the end of the 1870s, the dominion of Michael began. This has a quite different quality from that of Gabriel. Whereas, in the previous three centuries, one needed to seek for signs of archangelic dominion in the spiritual impulses which underpin the physical world, the rulership of Michael since then comes to expression primarily in all that relates to humanity's capacity for intelligence and reason—in other words, in all that affects humanity's intellectual and spiritual evolution and culture. In observing earthly humanity it is of extraordinary importance that the dominion of Gabriel, which one can say grasps hold of the most physical aspect of spirit, is always followed by the dominion of Michael, who is most connected with what we may call the spiritual aspects of culture. When we wish to find the archangel who stands guard over physical reproduction, then we gaze up to the archangel Gabriel; when, in contrast, we wish to seek the spirit who is connected with the development of intellectual pursuits and the arts, etc., then we look up to the archangel being who, in Christian tradition, is called Michael. The cultures and civilizations that are of prime importance in each age are always governed by a succession of seven archangels; and thus the dominion of Michael was preceded by six other periods in which different archangels held sway. When we look back further, before Gabriel, we then come again to a former age when Michael held dominion and influence over the earth. Each age of an archangel's dominion is always a recapitulation of earlier, similar periods, and the evolution of the archangels themselves occurs simultaneously by means of this onward development. Always, after a certain period of around two millennia, the same archangel comes to hold sway over the culture and civilization that is decisive in human evolution at the time.

But these periods of dominion, each of which lasts around three centuries or a little more, are markedly different from one another—not always as different as the Michael age and the Gabriel age, but nevertheless they are decidedly different. We can say that whenever Gabriel holds sway a subsequent period is in preparation when peoples will be sundered, divided and differentiated. This is an age when nations become more nationalistic. You might therefore ask why, now that the Michael age has dawned, such a strongly nationalistic streak is pervading civilization. Well, this is because it was in preparation for a long time beforehand; it then works on, and then slowly fades and leaves considerable after-pangs that are often worse than the age itself which caused them. Only gradually does the Michael impetus infuse what is still largely characteristic of Gabriel's rulership. But whenever the Michael age begins, a longing surfaces in earthly humanity to overcome all racial distinctions and divisions, and to spread across all the different peoples inhabiting the earth the highest spiritual content and culture arising in a certain epoch. Michael's dominion always invokes the spread of a cosmopolitan principle and the highest spiritual culture amongst nations and peoples—irrespective of their language—who are open to it. Thus of the seven archangels who bring their impulses to bear on human evolution, Michael is always the one who invokes a cosmopolitan impetus, and who at the same time kindles a desire to spread the most valuable qualities and cultural achievements of the age among human beings.

If we now trace back humanity's evolution and enquire into the last Michael age before our present one, we arrive at the epoch—founded on the most significant culture of that time, that of ancient Greece—whose conclusion witnessed the cosmopolitan deeds embodied in Alexander's military expeditions to Asia. There we find how, as though emerging from ancient cultural evolution, an urge arose to introduce oriental peoples to the spiritual culture of the small country of Greece, to bear this culture to Egypt and spread it in cosmopolitan fashion amongst all the people who were open to it at the time. It is enormously significant that this Michael age gave rise to a cosmopolitan impetus for spreading throughout humanity all that had been achieved by Greece. And when the city of Alexandria began to flourish in North Africa, this cultural blossoming was in a certain sense the crowning of that Michael age.

This was the last age of Michael, after which followed the other six archangel periods. And in the last third of the nineteenth century, at the end of the 1870s, a new Michael age began.

But never in the whole course of earthly evolution was there such a great difference between two successive Michael ages as between the time of Alexander and the epoch in which we have been living since the end of the 1870s. Between these two ages of Michael there falls, of course, the event which gave earthly evolution its true meaning: the Mystery of Golgotha.

Now we must recall what Michael really governs throughout the whole spiritual cosmos. He holds sway not only over what is spiritual, but over what must also culminate in human, intellectual understanding. Michael is not a spirit who simply nurtures intellectual acuity; all that he gives as spirituality aims, rather, to illumine humanity as ideas and thoughts which grasp the spirit. Michael wants the human being to be a free being who discerns in his concepts and ideas what comes to him as revelation from the world of spirit.

And now let us look at the Michael age at the time of Alexander. I have often said that people nowadays are very, very clever—they have intellectual concepts and ideas, and a self-developed intellectualism. But people in Alexander's day were also very clever. Yet if one had asked them at the time where they got their concepts and ideas from they would never have said that they acquired them by their own efforts. They felt that they received spiritual revelations—and with these their idea also. Thus they did not regard ideas as something one could form oneself, but rather as a revelation which came to them as part of their spiritual nature. And—in contrast to today's earthbound perspective—this was a heaven-sent intellectuality, over which Michael held sway at the time of Alexander. He was the most glorious of the archangels who indwell the sun. He was the spirit who not only sent physical-etheric sunrays out from the sun but also intellectual inspiration towards earth in these physical and etheric sunbeams. In those days people knew that what they developed on earth as the power of intelligence was a gift from heaven, from the sun, and was sent down to them from the sun. Michael, they knew, was the spirit in direct charge of this, who sent down intellectuality by spiritual means to the earth. This was also a teaching of the ancient sun mysteries: that Michael lives in the sun, that he holds sway there as cosmic intelligence inspiring people as a gift from Michael.

But now there followed the epoch when, increasingly, preparation was to be made for human beings developing intellect out of their own power of soul. They would no longer just receive the revelation of cosmic intelligence, but would become intelligent by their own powers. Aristotelianism laid the ground for this, arising at the twilight of ancient Greece as a remarkable, emerging philosophical view which gave the impetus for Alexander's military expeditions to Asia and Africa. Aristotelianism embodied, one can say, an emancipation or birth of earthly intelligence from the womb of cosmic intelligence. What was later called Aristotelian logic gave birth to an intellectual framework which subsequently became human intelligence in all succeeding centuries. And now you must consider that this founding of earthly, human intelligence, and the way it impacted as Greek culture on people of a cosmopolitan disposition, stands there, in the form of Alexander's campaigns, as a last deed originating from Michael impulses at the time. That was a unified deed.

Then the age of Oriphiel succeeded that of Michael. The

archangel Oriphiel held sway. The Mystery of Golgotha took place. The human souls who, under the rulership of Michael during the time of Alexander, had played a conscious part in the deeds I have spoken of, gathered around the archangel Michael within the sun at the outset of the Christian era. Michael had for the time being ceded his dominion to Oriphiel but, with those human souls who served him, he participated in Christ's departure from the sun.

And this too is something we must consider: that those human souls who together are connected with the anthroposophical movement had an inner sense that they were united with Michael on the sun and that Christ, who until then had sent his impulses down to earth from the sun, was departing from it in order to unite with earthly evolution. Just think, vividly, of this significant, supersensible and cosmic event, this special perspective vouchsafed to those souls who had gathered around after he completed his rulership on earth, as servants of the angeloi, and who as it were within the region of the sun participated in Christ's departure from the sun to unite his destiny with earthly humanity. 'He is leaving!' was the great experience they had.

Human souls really do not just acquire their impetus on earth, but also find orientation in the life between death and a new birth. This is primarily how it was for those who had witnessed the age of Alexander. A mighty impetus emanated from that great moment of cosmic and evolutionary importance when these souls saw that Christ was departing from the sun. And for them the fact was clear that cosmic intelligence was gradually passing from the cosmos to the earth. And one can say that Michael, and those gathered around him, saw how all the intelligence which formerly streamed from the cosmos gradually sank down onto the earth.

And Michael and those who belonged to him—whether they were up above in the world of spirit or were briefly incarnated below on earth—could see how the streams of intelligent life would arrive in the earthly sphere itself in the eighth Christian century, and knew that this intelligence would continue to unfold and develop there. And on earth it was possible to see the advent of the first real thinkers. The great minds of past eras had in fact received and possessed their ideas as inspirations. But now, from the eighth century AD, self-directed thinkers arose. And within the choir of archangels in the sun region the following mighty phrase resounded from Michael's being: 'What was once the power of my kingdom, which was governed through me from here, is no longer here; it must stream, surge and swell there below on the earth.'

From the eighth century onwards, this was the perspective as seen from the sun. This was also the great secret, that the powers which are primarily those of Michael descended from the heavens to the earth. This great secret was conveyed to some initiates in schools of the type I described yesterday, for example, the high school of Chartres. We could put it like this: previously, if one wished to know the nature of intelligence, one had to gaze upwards to the sun through the window of the mysteries. Intelligence now was not as visible as this on earth, but it gradually became known that people were evolving their own thinking on earth, their own intelligence. One of the first to show sparks in his soul of self-directed thinking was Johannes Scotus Erigena, whom I have often mentioned. But he was preceded by others who also already possessed their own thinking powers, and no longer just inspired thinking revealed to them from above. This internalized thinking increasingly made headway.

In Earth's evolution, however, particular use could be made of this self-directed thinking. Just consider for a moment that such self-directed thinking represented the sum of impulses which had descended from Michael's region to the earth. Michael was initially called upon to let this earthly intelligence continue to develop here on earth. He was not yet himself involved in it, and would only begin to be so again from 1879 onwards. This earthly thinking initially developed in a way that did not yet allow Michael to hold dominion over it. He was not yet able to give an impetus to self-directed thinkers, for his rulership, his epoch, had not yet arrived.

In a few of the oriental mystery centres people knew this deep secret of what now prevailed in humanity's evolution. In these particular oriental mysteries, deeply spiritual and highly schooled people were able to initiate a few pupils into this great secret. And in ways that are difficult to comprehend for ordinary earthly understanding, this secret, which was well known in a few oriental mystery centres, made itself felt in the illustrious court which I have mentioned at the Goetheanum and elsewhere. In the eighth and at the beginning of the ninth century, this court held sway in Asia under the rulership of Harun-al-Rashid. This figure was steeped in an Arab culture tinged with Mohammedanism. His advisers, who were either initiates themselves or had acquired a certain degree of knowledge, knew something of the secret I have mentioned. The Baghdad court of Harun-al-Rashid was so illustrious precisely because it was touched by this secret. Everything present in the Orient in the way of wisdom, art and deep religious feeling was focused and magnified at the court of Harun-al-Rashid—and somewhat tinged with Mohammedanism. In Europe at this time, at the court of Charlemagne, a contemporary of Harun-al-Rashid, people were preoccupied with compiling the basic elements of grammar, and things were still in a semi-barbarian state. Baghdad, in contrast, was the flourishing centre of spiritual life and culture in the Middle East. Harun-al-Rashid gathered around him those who knew about the great mystery traditions of the Orient. In particular he had one adviser who had been an initiate in former times, and on whom earlier incarnations still exerted a spiritual impetus. It was he who instilled everything in the way of geometry, chemistry, physics, music, architecture and other arts that were cultivated at Harun-al-Rashid's court, and in particular a glorious art of poetry. In this illustrious gathering of wise men at the court there prevailed a more or less conscious sense that the earth's intelligence, which had descended from the heavens to earth, must be placed at the service of the Mohammedan culture and spirit.

Now just consider that from the age of Mohammed onwards, from the era of the first caliphs, Arabism spread from Asia through North Africa and as far as Europe. There it continued to spread through wars. But those who spread Arabism by means of warfare, as far as Spain—France too was touched by it, and culturally the whole of western Europe—were accompanied by significant individuals. And you all know about the Crusades of the Frankish kings against the Moors, against Arabism. But that is only the external, historically recorded aspect. What is always much more important are the spiritual streams which unfold inwardly in human evolution.

Then both Harun-al-Rashid and his significant adviser passed through the gate of death. But after they died and entered their existence between death and a new life, in a strange and remarkable way they continued to pursue their aims of imbuing the European world with the Arab way of thinking, with the aid of the growing principle of intelligence. After Harun-al-Rashid had passed through death, therefore, we see how, as his soul passed through the starry worlds of spirit, its gaze continued to focus intently in a broad sweep from Asia, from Baghdad through Africa, Spain and via western Europe as far as England. Harun-al-Rashid's soul continued to direct its gaze upon Greece and Rome, on Spain and France, and all the way to England. His life between death and a new birth was focused continually on the south and west of Europe. And then Harun-al-Rashid appeared again in a new incarnation—and he became Lord Bacon of Verulam. Bacon was indeed Harun-al-Rashid, and in the intervening period between death and a new birth he exerted the influence I have described. But the other individual, his wise adviser, chose the other path: from Baghdad through the Black Sea and Russia to Central Europe. These two individualities took two different directions: Harun-al-Rashid passed on to his next earthly goal as Lord Bacon, while the wise adviser, during his life between death and a new birth, never turned his gaze from the influence that can increasingly be exerted and instilled from the East. He appeared again as the great educational reformer and author of the 'Pan-Sophia', as Amos Comenius (Komenski). And in Europe, through the collaboration of these two individuals who had once held sway in the Baghdad court, there developed—more or less irrespective of Christianity—an antiquated Arabism, under the influence of what one can call an intelligence sundered from Michael and the sun.

What occurred outwardly in the form of wars was repelled by the Frankish kings and other Europeans. We can observe how the Arab campaigns, which initially have such an impetus and spread Mohammedan culture, collapse in the West and penetrate no further. We see how Mohammedanism vanishes from western Europe. But even as it shed its outer forms, and all that it had established as external culture, this Arabism assumed a more modern form in natural science, developing into what Amos Comenius established in the field of education. Thus, in the seventeenth century, earthly intelligence that had fallen under the sway and occupation, as it were, of Arabism, continued to spread.

As such we find the soil into which, today, we need to sow the seed of anthroposophy. We really need to consider this in its inner spiritual significance.

Whereas, coming from Asia, the illustrious court at Baghdad was perpetrated spiritually, Christianity was spreading in Europe. But the spread of Aristotelianism in Europe was, one may say, fraught with the greatest difficulties. The great deeds of Alexander had borne Aristotelianism towards Asia as natural science, through everything which had developed in a mighty way from the Hellenistic culture of Greece, and this was then taken over or 'occupied' by Arabism. In Europe, on the other hand, what one may call a thin veneer of Aristotelianism was spreading within the expanding Christian culture, where it connected and united with Platonism, which was absolutely rooted in the ancient Greek mysteries.

But initially we see how Aristotelianism spread very tentatively in Europe, whereas Platonism took on more salient form in the schools that were founded. And one of the most important of these was the School of Chartres in the twelfth century, in which the great scholars were active whom I mentioned yesterday: Bernard Sylvestris, Bernard of Chartres, John of Salisbury and, foremost among them,

Alanus ab Insulis. In this Chartres School things were expressed differently from the way they were embodied in the waning echo of Arabism. At the School of Chartres lived authentic Christianity, but illumined by the ancient mysteries, by the wisdom that could still be drawn from them.

And then something very significant occurred. Those great teachers of Chartres who were far removed from Arabism but whose Platonism had become deeply imbued with the secrets of Christianity, passed through the gate of death. And at this time, at the beginning of the thirteenth century, a great, heavenly council was held. Once the greatest of the scholars had died, first and foremost Alanus ab Insulis, and were therefore in the world of spirit, they gathered together to enact a significant cosmic deed in collaboration with those who were also there still in the spiritual world and were about to descend to earth and there embody Aristotelianism in a new way. And these souls about to descend included ones who had participated during the time of Alexander in the workings of the Michael impetus, and had done so with intense and inmost strength of soul. And because it corresponds with the truth, we can imagine that at this turning point from the twelfth to the thirteenth centuries there came together souls who, on the one hand, had just arrived in the world of spirit from centres of Christian initiation such as the School of Chartres, and those who were preparing to descend to a new incarnation and who had preserved in spiritual regions not Platonism but Aristotelianism—the inner impetus of intelligence that still drew on the old epoch of Michael. These said to themselves: 'We were gathered around Michael, and with him witnessed how intelligence streamed down to earth from the heavens; we were united with him also in the great cosmopolitan deed which was accomplished under the old dispensation of Michael, when intelligence still streamed from him.'

And thus the teachers of the Chartres School for the time being passed to the Aristotelians the power of dispensation over spiritual matters on earth. In other words, the Platonists ceded dispensation over spiritual life on earth to those preparing to descend to earth—who were particularly suited to overseeing living, self-directed earthly intelligence. The Platonists, on the other hand, could really only admit the kind of influence whereby intelligence is dispensed 'from the heavens'.

These descending spirits, in whose souls there resonated an echo of the Michael impetus from the previous Michael age, entered the Dominican orders in particular. And, arising from the Dominican order, there developed the school of Scholasticism which wrestled acerbically but also magnificently with the question of the nature of intelligent thinking. This was really the great question rooted in the depths of the souls of the founders of Scholasticism in the thirteenth century: the burning question about Michael's further dominion.

Here there were people who were later called the nominalists. These believed that concepts and ideas are merely names or identifiers, have no intrinsic reality. This group was influenced by Ahriman, for the nominalists really wished to banish Michael's dominion from the earth. By claiming that ideas were merely names and nothing real in themselves, they wished to prevent Michael's influence from exerting its effect on earth. And the ahrimanic spirits said to those who had an ear for it: cosmic intelligence has fallen away from Michael, and is now active here on earth. Let us prevent Michael from regaining dominion over intelligence! Yet the plan of the heavenly council I referred to was precisely that Platonists and Aristotelians together conceived a plan to enable the Michael impulses to continue to take effect. The nominalists were opposed by the Dominican realists, who said: 'Ideas and thoughts are real; they live and are embodied in things. They are not mere names.'

If one has understanding for this, one can sometimes be reminded of such things in a really remarkable, striking way. During my last years in Vienna I became acquainted with, among others, a priest belonging to a religious order. This was Vincenz Knauer who wrote the philosophical treatise I have often advised anthroposophists to read, *Hauptprobleme der Philosophie* ['Major problems in philosophy']. In the nineteenth century he was still preoccupied with this dispute between the nominalists and realists, and tried to show that nominalism is based on a fundamental error. To do so he chose a good example—and you can also find this in his books. But I recall with profound satisfaction the time when we were walking together along the Währinger Strasse in Vienna and discussing nominalism and realism, and—with the full force of his circumspect enthusiasm, which was very remarkable, having something of the quality of honest philosophical enquiry whereas most other philosophers had lost this to a greater or lesser extent—he said: 'I always tell my students that what lives as ideas within things has reality, and I ask them to consider a lamb and a wolf. In relation to these the nominalists would say that the lamb is constituted of muscles, bones and matter; and the wolf, likewise, of muscles, bones and matter. What is realized as form, as the idea of the lamb in lamb flesh, is just a name. "Lamb" is a name, is not real as an idea. The same is true of the wolf. As idea it has no reality, but is merely a name. But it is easy to refute the nominalists,' said dear Knauer, 'for one just has to show them the following. If you were to give a wolf no food for a while other than lamb's flesh then, if the "idea" of lamb has no reality, is nothing but a name, and if the matter in the lamb is all it consists of, then the wolf would gradually but inevitably turn into a lamb. It does not do so however! On the contrary, it retains its wolf reality. In what we see before us as lamb, therefore, the idea of lamb has as it were drawn matter to itself and clothed it in form; and the same is true of the wolf—the idea of wolf attracts matter and creates its appropriate form.'

But basically it was this dispute that waged between the nominalists and realists: it concerned the reality of what can be grasped through intelligence.

Thus the Dominicans had to prepare the way, at the due time, for Michael's next period of rulership. And whereas the Platonists, for instance the teachers of the Chartres School, remained in the world of spirit after the resolution taken by this heavenly council at the beginning of the thirteenth century, and had no significant incarnations, the Aristotelians were to promote intelligence on earth. From Scholasticism— which only in the modern era was so distorted, caricatured and ahrimanized by Rome—emanated all modern intellectual striving, in so far as it remained free of the Arabist influence.

At this period in central and western Europe, therefore, we see these two streams: the one with which Bacon and Amos Comenius are connected; and the Scholastic stream, involving cultivation of Christian Aristotelianism's spiritual evolution in culture, in preparation for a new Michael age. When, during the dominion of former archangels, the Scholastics sought to gaze up to regions of spirit, they told themselves that Michael was there, that they had to wait for his era to come, but that they had to prepare for what he must, at the due time, one day again take upon himself. This, they knew, had fallen away from him for now, in accordance with the needs of cosmic evolution. Thus a stream developed which, though falsely diverted in Catholic Ultramontanism, continued to flow, perpetuating what was first established in the thirteenth century.

In other words, this stream drew directly on Aristotelianism to embody earthly intelligence. There also lived in it what I spoke of yesterday, when I said that one soul remained somewhat longer with Alanus ab Insulis in the world of spirit, descending then as a younger Dominican and bringing to an older Dominican who had descended to earth before him a message from Alanus ab Insulis. An intense will prevailed at the time in Europe's spiritual life to take a strong hold on ideas. And in realms above the earth all this then also gave rise to what, at the beginning of the nineteenth century, led to a great, encompassing act in the spiritual world where what was later to become anthroposophy unfolded in mighty imaginations. In the first half of the nineteenth century, and already briefly at the end of the eighteenth, all those who were Platonists led by the teachers of Chartres, who were now passing between death and a new birth, and also those who established Aristotelianism in Europe—and in the meantime had also long since passed through the gate of death—were gathered together in heavenly regions to perform a supersensible rite and sacrament. Here, in mighty, living imaginations was summoned what was to be re-established in the new Christianity of the twentieth century in a spiritual way, after the new Michael age had begun in the last third of the nineteenth century.

A good deal of this filtered through to earth. Up above, in worlds of spirit, the preparation for that intelligent but certainly also spiritual entity that was to appear as anthroposophy was unfolding in mighty, cosmic imaginations. What filtered through made a particular impression on Goethe. One can say that it surfaced in him in miniature images. Goethe was unaware of the mighty images that unfolded above, but he integrated these miniatures into his *Fairy Tale of the Green Snake and the Beautiful Lily.* A wonderful phenomenon! We have here the whole power of the streams I described, continuing in such a way that they lead to those mighty imaginations unfolding above in the spiritual world under the guidance of Alanus ab Insulis and others. And then we have the mighty fact that these things filter down and inspire Goethe, at the cusp between the eighteenth and nineteenth centuries, to write his spiritual *Fairy Tale of the Green Snake and the Beautiful Lily.* This was the first earthly emergence of what unfolded at the beginning of the nineteenth and already at the end of the eighteenth century in mighty imaginations in the world of spirit. You will therefore not be surprised to learn that my first Mystery play, *The Portal of Initiation,* which in a certain sense aimed to reflect the supersensible rite that occurred at the beginning of the nineteenth century, has certain outward similarities of structure with what Goethe portrayed in his *Fairy Tale of the Green Snake and the Beautiful Lily.* Having lived in supersensible regions in the form of imaginations, anthroposophy was to descend to earthly regions. Something occurred at this time in super-earthly realms: a great number of souls whom Christianity had touched at various ages united with souls who had been less connected with Christianity, who had been living at the time the Mystery of Golgotha took place on the earth, and prior to that. These two groups of souls united to prepare anthroposophy in super-earthly realms. Those I have described, gathered around Alanus ab Insulis, and those in the Dominican stream who had established Aristotelianism in Europe, also united with Dante's great teacher Brunetto Latini. And this great gathering of souls included a large number of those who today, having descended again to earth, join together in the Anthroposophical Society. The people who today feel drawn to work within the Anthroposophical Society were gathered in supersensible regions at the beginning of the nineteenth century in order to perform that mighty imaginal rite which I have described.

This is also something linked to the karma of the anthroposophical movement. It is something we meet when we do not just consider this anthroposophical movement in rationalistic terms, in its external form on earth, but when we also trace back the threads which lead up into regions of spirit. Then we can see how the anthroposophical movement descends as it were. Yes, at the end of the eighteenth and beginning of the nineteenth century we have the 'heavenly' anthroposophic movement; it filters through into what Goethe portrays in miniature in the *The Fairy Tale of the Green Snake and the Beautiful Lily*. But then it must descend more fully when, in the last third of the nineteenth century, Michael descends from the sun to the earth and tries to grasp hold of human earthly intelligence.

From the Mystery of Golgotha onwards, Christ was united with earthly humanity. Humanity on earth could not initially grasp him outwardly. Michael's rulership oversaw the last phase of cosmic intelligence during the age of Alexander. With the eighth century AD, cosmic intelligence had fallen entirely to the earth. After reaching an understanding with the Platonists, those who were bound to Michael then undertook to prepare this earth intelligence in Scholastic realism in such a way that Michael could once again unite with it when he embarked on his new era at the end of the 1870s, as part of civilization's ongoing evolution.

What matters now is that the Anthroposophical Society should grasp this inner task, which consists in making way for Michael in human thinking and not contesting his influence. We mustn't be fatalistic. We can only say that people have to collaborate with the gods. Michael inspires human beings with his own being so that a spirituality can appear on earth which is equal to people's own personal intelligence—so that we can both think and be spiritual human beings; for this is the real meaning of Michael's dominion. We have to fight for this within the anthroposophical movement. And then those who today work to further the anthroposophical movement will reappear again at the end of the twentieth century, and on earth will be deeply connected with those who were once the teachers of Chartres. For this was the understanding reached by that heavenly council at the beginning of the thirteenth century: that the Aristotelians and Platonists would appear together, and work to cultivate the anthroposophical movement in ever more flourishing ways in the twentieth century, so that at the end of that century anthroposophy can achieve a certain culmination in earthly civilization, through the joint forces of the Platonists and Aristotelians. If such work can be accomplished, as predestined by Michael, then Europe, modern civilization, will arise from decline. But in no other way will this happen! Leading civilization out of its decadence is connected with acquiring understanding of Michael.

I have thus led you, my dear friends, to insight into the Mystery of Michael which holds sway in our present time over thinking and spiritually striving humanity. You will understand that anthroposophy must incorporate into spiritual evolution something that appears paradoxical to many, for all kinds of demonic, ahrimanic powers are possessing human beings. In many human bodies the ahrimanic powers have already rejoiced at the possibility that Michael may no longer be able to sustain his cosmic intelligence that has fallen to the earth. Such rejoicing was particularly jubilant in the middle of the nineteenth century when Ahriman already believed that Michael would not recover his former cosmic intelligence, which had made its way from the heavens to earth. Things of immense importance are at stake here! It is therefore hardly surprising if the souls locked in these battles have to experience some strange things.

Never before have such strange things been said about a spiritual movement as are said about the anthroposophical movement. This strange way of speaking about it tells us that its spiritual character and its connection with the Mystery of Golgotha cannot be grasped by some of the most enlightened minds of our day. Would anyone say, for example, that he'd seen someone who was simultaneously black *and* white? You would hardly credit the sanity of someone who said such a thing. Yet today people write similar things about the anthroposophic movement. In his book *The Great Secret*,[4] Maurice Maeterlinck elaborates a kind of logic when speaking of me as the prime mover of the anthroposophical movement, which is really tantamount to saying something is black and white simultaneously—a logical impossibility. Let me quote what Maeterlinck says:

What we read in the Vedas, says Rudolf Steiner—one of the most learned and also muddle-headed of contemporary occultists...

You see, he can get away with writing this despite the fact that it is intrinsically contradictory. And he continues:

Rudolf Steiner, when he does not lose himself in visions of prehistory—which are plausible perhaps but unverifiable, in astral jargon about life on other planets, is in fact a very clear and shrewd thinker, who has illuminated the meaning of this judgement [he is referring here to 'osirification' in ancient Egypt] with extraordinary clarity.

In other words, Maeterlinck is saying that this man is a shrewd, clear thinker as long as he does not speak about anthroposophy. Maeterlinck permits himself to say this. But he goes still further, as follows:

Steiner has applied his intuitive methods, which consist of a kind of psychometry, in order to reconstruct the history of the Atlanteans and to reveal to us what occurs on the sun, the moon and other worlds. He describes to us the successive transformations of the beings who become the human being, and he does so with such assurance that one has to ask, after following him with interest through his introduction—which is very balanced, logical and wide-ranging—whether he has suddenly gone mad; or whether we are dealing with a hoaxer or genuine visionary.

Just reflect for a moment on what this means. Maeterlinck claims that whenever I write books the introductions always appear to testify to a 'very balanced, logical and wide-ranging' mind. But when he reads further in my books he no longer knows whether I have suddenly gone mad or whether I am a hoaxer or genuine seer. But I have written quite a number of books, and I always first write the introduction. Very well then ... I write a book and Maeterlinck reads the introduction, and he finds me to be a 'very balanced, logical and wind-ranging' mind. But then he reads on and finds me different, and begins to wonder whether I'm mad, or a hoaxer or visionary. And so it goes on ... I write a second book, and when Maeterlinck reads the new introduction he again finds me well-balanced and so forth, but once again the further content strikes him as crazy. And this could continue indefinitely. But to say this would make me a very strange creature indeed, first sensible, balanced and logical—but then suddenly mad! And then, in the next book logical once more, and then suddenly mad again. On and on like this, in a rhythmical kind of fashion. Well, there are rhythmic alternations in the world I suppose!

But this example can show how the most enlightened minds of today fail to recognize what must be established as Michael epoch in the world, and what must be accomplished so that the cosmic intelligence which quite properly fell away from Michael in the eighth century, in accordance with evolutionary needs, can be rediscovered within humanity on earth. The whole Michael tradition must be renewed—Michael, with his feet upon the dragon. It is right to contemplate this picture, portraying Michael the warrior as he embodies the cosmic spirit in opposition to the ahrimanic powers pinned beneath his feet.

More than any other battle, this battle is inscribed in the human heart. There it has been rooted since the last third of the nineteenth century. What human hearts make of this Michael impulse during the course of the twentieth century must and will be decisive. And during this twentieth century, as the first century after the end of Kali Yuga elapses, humanity will either stand at the grave of all civilization or at the beginning of an age when human souls come to unite intelligence with spirituality in their hearts, and the outcome of the Michael battle allows the Michael impetus to unfold fully.

5. *Hearts Inscribed in the Michael School*

Lecture given at Arnhem on 20 July 1924

You will have seen from what I said yesterday about the spiritual, cosmic aspect of Michael's dominion that Michael holds a special place amongst those spiritual beings we call (in accordance with old Christian traditions) the Archangeloi. And because of its central bearing on the theme of these lectures, we can recognize the importance of the fact that, in the centuries before Christianity was founded, Michael sent out his impulses to earth from the sun, from the solar region—what I'd like to call his cosmopolitan impulses; and that these cosmopolitan impulses were lost, that cosmic intelligence sank away from Michael as it were, and arrived on earth in the eighth century AD. We then find people in the earth's evolution who can think for themselves, direct their own thinking; and this self-directed thinking was then cultivated and striven for in a way that would make a further Michael era possible. As I showed yesterday, this was accomplished by the wise leaders of the School of Chartres in harmonious collaboration with those drawn from the old period of Michael's dominion, who were predestined to continue to cultivate the principle of the former cosmic and now earthly intelligence until, in the nineteenth century, the possibility arrived to prepare what would one day become the aims of the anthroposophical movement. This preparation occurred in the world of spirit initially, through that rite of mighty imaginations which I described to you. Since the last third of the nineteenth century but particularly now, in our time, we stand at the beginning of the new rule of Michael. This Michael dominion will prepare what must still take place this century: a larger number of people—precisely those who develop a real understanding of anthroposophy—will need to pass through the period between death and a new birth in a more rapid way before the end of the century, and, returning to earth, unite under the leadership of what one may call both types of spiritual orientation, the teachers of Chartres and those who remained directly united with Michael's dominion. Under the leadership of both these types of spiritual being, these souls will then need to give, if I may put it like this, the final, hallowed impetus for the further development of spiritual life on earth.

For those who wish to participate in it, anthroposophy will only be able to gain real significance if they become aware, with a certain inner, holy zeal, that they can stand within the kind of context that I characterized yesterday. This will kindle inner enthusiasm, and also strength. This will allow us to know that we need to work towards becoming, increasingly, souls who continue and develop what once lived in the ancient mysteries.

Such awareness has to be intensified and deepened in all directions. And this can happen. In the light of what we said yesterday, we can look back to the time when Michael was united in the spiritual solar region with a number of super-earthly beings, and sent down to earth from this spiritual sun-sphere signs which, on the one hand, inspired the deeds of Alexander, and on the other kindled Aristotelian philosophy. These represented, one can say, the final phase of inspired, spiritual intelligence on earth. Then, from the sun, with those human souls who had accomplished these things on earth on his behalf, as it were, Michael observed the Mystery of

Golgotha with his spiritual hosts and the hosts of human souls who gathered around such leading human individuals. And we can indeed imbue ourselves with a quality that spurs the soul if we imagine the moment when Michael, with a host of angels, archangels and human souls, sees Christ depart from the sun and enter the physical habitation of a human being, so as to unite with humanity's further evolution on earth through what he can experience in a human body on earth. For Michael, however, this was simultaneously the sign that from then on the heavenly intelligence he had so far safeguarded must stream down to earth, like holy rain, and fall away from the sun. And in the eighth century AD, those who were gathered around Michael saw how the substance so far preserved by Michael had finally arrived upon earth.

Then, in complete harmony with Michael's sovereignty, it was necessary for everything to emerge in the world which came about through the masters of Chartres and also through those in the Dominican orders who were chosen for this. Briefly, humanity's evolution was to be led, from the beginning of the fifteenth century, towards development of the consciousness soul—a development that still continues today. Roughly in the first third of the preceding epoch, that is in the first third of the age of the intellectual or mind soul, we see the spread of super-earthly intelligence across Asia, Africa and part of Europe, carried by Alexander's impetus. But now a special era arrives, one in which Michael in the sun, the most illustrious archangel spirit, shows us that he knows his dispensation of cosmic intelligence has departed from the sun, and that conditions are now such that the further development of this intelligence can continue on earth. This era arrives around the sixteenth and seventeenth centuries AD. Here one can say that Michael is released from his former obligations in the cosmos, and Gabriel instead oversees earthly evolution, in the way I described yesterday.

Michael was now in an unusual position. Whenever an archangel is not holding sway over earthly concerns, he allows his impetus, instead, to flow into whatever another archangel does, for such impetuses flow continually from all seven successively ruling archangels. One predominates, that is all. For example, when Gabriel was the prevailing spirit in former epochs of humanity's evolution, what flowed into earthly evolution came predominantly from him, but the other archangels participated in it too. But now, as Gabriel held sway, Michael was in the unusual position of being unable to affect earthly concerns from the sun. This is most unusual for a ruling archangel: to see that his activity and influence, exerted through long ages, has more or less ceased. And thus Michael said to those who belonged to him: 'It is necessary for the period during which we cannot send impulses to the earth—a period which is to end around 1879—that we seek out a particular task within the sun-sphere.' This meant that for those souls whose karma would lead them to the anthroposophical movement there should be the possibility of looking towards the sun region to see what Michael and his spirits were doing while Gabriel's influence was predominant on earth.

This was something exceptional in all the other regularly recurring deeds of gods and men. The souls connected with Michael—the leading souls of the Alexander period, those of the great Dominican era, those who had assembled round them in less of a leading role, and a large number of striving, developing human beings in conjunction with the leading spirits—felt as though torn out of their traditional context and connection with the world of spirit. The human souls

who were predestined to become anthroposophists experienced something in the supersensible realms that had never
previously been experienced in supersensible realms by
human souls passing between death and a new birth. In the
past, the experience between death and a new birth involved
souls working out their karma for their future existence on
earth, in conjunction with leading, guiding spiritual beings.
But karma had never before been worked out in the way that
now occurred for those predestined, by what has been
described, to become anthroposophists. Never before had
souls worked in the sun-sphere between death and a new
birth in the way that they now worked under the sovereignty
of Michael, who had been released from involvement in
earthly matters.

Something occurred then as an event in supersensible
regions which today lies in the profound, innermost depths of
the heart of most anthroposophists—though unconscious,
wrapped in dream, asleep. And the anthroposophist, touch-
ing into his heart, is right to say, 'Within me is a secret,
perhaps unconscious: a reflection of Michael's deeds in the
super-earthly regions in the sixteenth, seventeenth and
eighteenth centuries when, before I descended again to my
present life on earth, I worked under Michael's guidance. At
that time he could achieve something unusual because he
had, as it were, been released from his ongoing tasks.'

Michael gathered his hosts, those who belonged to him as
supersensible beings from the regions of the Angeloi and
Archangeloi; he also gathered human souls who had formed
some kind of connection with him. And in this way there
arose something like a mighty, expanding, supersensible
school. Just as those who could work together as Platonists
and Aristotelians had held a kind of heavenly council at the

beginning of the thirteenth century, so now, under Michael's direction, a supersensible schooling took place from the fifteenth to the eighteenth centuries, with Michael himself assigned as its great teacher by cosmic decree. Thus what I have told you in relation to the first half of the nineteenth century, of the supersensible rite conjured in mighty imaginations, was preceded by a supersensible schooling for numerous human souls—a schooling whose fruits these human souls now bear unconsciously within them. The fruits of this schooling only emerge in the urge of these souls towards anthroposophy. This urge to find anthroposophy results from that schooling. In fact we can say that at the end of the fifteenth century, Michael assembled his hosts of gods and human souls in the region of the sun and addressed them in a speech which continued over long periods, and whose content was roughly as follows:

> *Since the human race has populated the earth in human form, there have been mysteries on the earth: sun mysteries, Mercury, Venus, Mars, Jupiter and Saturn mysteries. The gods have sent their secrets into these mysteries, and human beings suited to this have been initiated there. Thus people on earth have been able to know what occurs on Saturn, Jupiter, Mars and so forth, and how what occurs there works into human evolution on earth. There have always been initiates who communicated with the gods through the mysteries. Through the old, instinctive clairvoyance such initiates absorbed the impulses which penetrated to them through the mysteries. Except for a few residual traditions, this has now vanished from the earth and is no longer present. Such impetus can no longer flow into the earth. Only in the very lowest region, that of reproduction, does Gabriel still have the power to let moon*

influences enter humanity's evolution. The ancient traditions have more or less vanished from the earth, and with them the possibility of cultivating the impulses entering the subconscious and thereby also the various bodies of human beings. We look back however to all that was once given to human beings in the mysteries as a gift of heaven, we gaze upon this wonderful tableau, and look down upon the cycles of the ages. There we find the mystery centres, and see how heavenly wisdom streamed into the mysteries, how human beings were initiated by it, how from our consecrated realm in the sun the cosmic intelligence flowed down to human beings in such a way that humanity's great teachers received ideas, thoughts and concepts that were spiritual, that were given them as inspiration from our hallowed sun region. This has all vanished from the earth. We can see these things when we look back to ancient epochs of the earth: we see it gradually disappear from the earth through the period of Alexander and the subsequent reverberations of this period. Below we see, instead, an intelligence that has grown earthly gradually spreading amongst human beings. But nevertheless we retain this perspective, this gaze upon the secrets in which people were once initiated through the mysteries. Let us bring it to awareness! Let us bring it to the awareness of those spiritual beings around me who never appear in an earthly body but live only in etheric form. And let us also bring it to the awareness of those souls who often dwelt on earth in human bodies and are there at this moment and belong to the community of Michael; let us bring it to the awareness of these human souls. Let us gather and configure the great teachings of the initiates which once streamed down to earth in the old way through the mysteries; let us configure these teachings before the souls of those whose intelligence was connected with Michael.

And then, if I may use a very mundane and, in this context, seemingly almost trivial-sounding expression, this ancient initiation wisdom was 'studied'. A great, encompassing heavenly school came about in which Michael taught what he himself could no longer dispense. This was something vast and mighty, something which profoundly troubled the ahrimanic demons on earth, especially in the fifteenth, sixteenth and seventeenth centuries, and into the eighteenth century. It made them terribly agitated and this led to something remarkable. Something unfolded in polar opposition to the heavenly deeds occurring at this time. Above, in the world of spirit, was a lofty school that reconfigured the ancient initiation wisdom in supersensible realms and raised it anew into the intelligent awareness, the consciousness soul of, initially, the human souls predestined for this between death and a new birth. In a new way, this school raised up what in former times had lived in the mind soul, or also sentient soul, as treasures of wisdom. In inner words, addressed by Michael to those gathered round him in a way which in many respects appears stern, he taught them about universal and cosmic contexts, about anthroposophical contexts. These souls received a teaching which unveiled universal secrets. But at the same time, below on earth, the ahrimanic spirits were at work. And here it becomes necessary to point in direct and unvarnished fashion to a secret truth. From an external perspective this will quite certainly jar with contemporary civilization, yet it is a divine secret which anthroposophists must know if they are to properly guide civilization towards the end of the twentieth century in the way I have suggested is needed.

While Michael was schooling his hosts up above, a kind of sub-earthly ahrimanic school was founded below the earth's surface. Thus we can imagine two schools: the super-earthly Michael school, and then, directly below our feet—for in the sub-earthly realm spiritual forces also work and are active— an opposing ahrimanic school. Whereas no impetus streamed down from Michael at this time to inspire intelligence in a heavenly way, since intelligence was for the time being left to its own devices, the ahrimanic hosts strove all the more to send up impulses from below into human evolution. We can try to vividly conjure this mighty picture. Imagine it like this: the surface of the earth, then Michael above, teaching his hosts, revealing to them in universal words of great grandeur what the ancient initiation wisdom consisted of; and then, in opposition to this, the ahrimanic school in the subterranean regions of the earth, while on the earth itself the intelligence that has fallen away from heaven is developing. Michael here dispenses his teachings in heavenly isolation initially, sending no streams downwards from above, while the ahrimanic powers send their impulses up from below with all the more force.

In the centuries I am referring to there were, in fact, embodied souls who sensed the sinister nature of this situation. If you trace the cultural and spiritual history of Europe at this period, you can discover, remarkably, that people— sometimes very simple souls—had an uneasy sense of this: a sense that humanity had been abandoned by Michael's powers, and was instead subject to these demonic impulses rising like a spiritual haze from below and attempting to hold intelligence in thrall.

It is remarkable how closely interwoven with the human being must be the revelations of wisdom, if all that springs from them is to be beneficial. This is, in fact, the secret truth we must touch upon here. Someone whose task it is to proclaim Michaelic wisdom feels, in a certain sense, that he has found the right stance when he struggles to find the expression, the formulation in words, for the nature of Michael's wisdom. He even feels he occupies the right stance when he writes down this Michael wisdom so that it passes through his hands. For then what is spiritually connected with the human being flows as it were into the form of what he writes, into what he does. But it engenders an uneasy feeling when we see such writing—gladly communicated as reading matter, as Michaelic wisdom—being mechanically reproduced in the form of printed books. We have to endure this, and it belongs to our time. But this uneasy feeling towards printed matter is definitely felt by someone whose communications flow from the life of spirit.

After yesterday's lecture someone asked me whether—as Swedenborg already suggested—the letter might not be the last resonance of the living spirit. It is indeed! It remains so, at least, for as long as it flows from the spirit in continual, ongoing motion through a human being. But it becomes an ahrimanic power of spirit when mechanically fixed, when it appears before human beings as printed letter. For this is the strange thing—that it was this ahrimanic school, which was founded as counter-school to the Michael school and worked in the fifteenth, sixteenth, seventeenth and eighteenth centuries, which gave rise to the art of printing with all that ensued from it. This art of printing is the breeding ground from which can spring the demonic powers best able to combat Michael's dominion.

As anthroposophists we must be able to discern the real significance of things, their reality. In the art of printing we can recognize a spiritual power, but one, in fact, which Ahriman uses in opposition to Michael. This was the reason for Michael's continual warning to those whom he was teaching in his school, that when they returned to earth to realize what had been given them as inner disposition they should communicate the most important things by word of mouth, and not regard the 'literary' impact of the printed book as the most important thing. More intimate, face-to-face interpersonal connection is thus essentially closer to the direction of Michael's activity. Instead of just spreading the word through books, we need to gather together and absorb the most important impetuses through personal human contact. At the same time also—for otherwise Ahriman would gain huge power over us if we did not also make use of his arts—we must use printing, but only as it were to supply 'memory aids', to have something that takes account of the ahrimanic Zeitgeist. We should not try to eradicate printed books but instead give them the right relationship with what works directly and humanly, and then we can inaugurate what should flow through the Anthroposophical Society as Michael stream, subtly and imponderably to begin with.

It would be wrong to take what I have said as the basis for suggesting we should get rid of anthroposophical books! This would merely deliver up the printing media to the greatest enemies of Michael wisdom, and would render impossible the further spread of our anthroposophical work, which needs to flourish now and grow to the end of the twentieth century. Instead we must ennoble the art of printing through a reverent stance towards what lives in Michael wisdom. For what does Ahriman aim to achieve through printing in relation to Michael? What he wants—and we see this springing up everywhere—is to conquer intelligence and hold it in thrall, and to do so in a way that especially tries to intervene wherever conditions offer an opportunity for it.

What is the prime activity of the ahrimanic spirits in combating the forthcoming age of Michael? Their most salient and effective influence is in 'possessing' human beings wherever human consciousness is dulled—to intervene in human awareness. In 1914, many people whose consciousness was dimmed were thus implicated in the start of the devastating world war. The hosts of Ahriman waged this world war in such people's dulled awareness, using human beings for their purposes. We will never fully trace the origins of this war in an external way, by examining the archive documentation. Instead we have to look at history with clear vision and see that in various places there were decisive figures whose consciousness had been dulled. This was an opportunity for Ahriman to take possession of them. And if we want to know how easily Ahriman can possess people today, we need think only, for instance, of what happened when Europeans arrived in America with their printed works, at the time when native Americans still lived in eastern North America. When the Indians saw these strange symbols in the possession of the Europeans, they thought that they were small demons. They had the right kind of eye for this: they were extremely alarmed by all these small demons, a, b, etc., and the form they assumed in printed works. In these letters, reproduced in the most varied ways, lies something fascinating for modern people; and only the good stance towards Michael, which can see the directly human aspect of wisdom and its communication, will lead us beyond this enthralling fascination.

Yet bad things can happen here. I'd like to say the following to you. There are certain secrets of the cosmos which we can only penetrate once we have reached a fairly advanced age. If we possess initiation knowledge, each stage of life allows us to perceive various different secrets of existence. Between the age of 21 and 42, therefore, we can gaze upon sun conditions—but not before then. Between the age of 42 and 49, we can have vision of the Mars secrets, and between 49 and 56 we can perceive the Jupiter secrets. If one wishes to see the whole interconnection between cosmic secrets, however, one has to be at least 63. That is why I could not previously have talked of some things I can now speak of quite freely. If one wishes to understand what specifically relates to the Michael secrets, which work down from the sun-sphere, then one has to be able to look up from earth into cosmic secrets through Saturn wisdom, and must be able to sense that glimmering dawn in the world of spirit—and live within it—which emanates from Oriphiel who holds sway over Saturn. He was the ruling archangel at the time of the Mystery of Golgotha, and will become so once again after the end of the Michael age.

If one does so, shocking, devastating truths about our present times are revealed. For as consequence of the spread of printing across the globe, due to the ahrimanic school opposing the school of Michael, literary authorship has arisen widely. Before printing was invented, who were the authors? They were people who could really only disseminate their manuscripts in the most intimate circles, and in ones which were ready to receive such writings. How many hands did a book pass through before printing became widespread? We can gauge this if we consider that a kind of surrogate printing had been developed to a great degree of perfection in ancient Chinese culture. A form of printing had been developed then, at a time when Michael also held sway above and an ahrimanic counter-school worked below. But nothing special came of it. Ahriman was not yet powerful and was not in a position to attempt in any real way to wrest dominion over intelligence from Michael. This attempt was renewed again at the time of Alexander, but again was not successful.

But in the modern art of printing ahrimanism really came into its own; literary authorship became widespread. And something became possible—and is on the one hand as wonderful, brilliant and dazzling as, on the other, we must take it in our stride and not be over-awed by it, must assess it in a balanced way in its proper significance. First attempts have been made which we can describe, from the perspective of the sphere of Michael, as Ahriman's publication as an author! In Michael's circles this is regarded as a significant event. Ahriman has appeared as author! It is not just that people have been possessed by him, as I suggested in relation to the outbreak of war, but that Ahriman has himself appeared as author by communicating directly through human souls. We should not be surprised that he is a brilliant writer, for he is a great, encompassing spirit. He is, though, the spirit who, rather than aiding humanity's evolution on earth as the good gods desire it, works to counter this evolution. In his own domain he is not just a thoroughly serviceable power, but also a benevolent one. Those beings who are benevolent at one level of the world order are extraordinarily harmful at another. We should not assume, therefore, that Ahriman's works should be rejected. If we are aware of what is going on here we can even admire them. But we must perceive their ahrimanic character.

Michael teaches us to perceive this today, if we try to hearken to him. The Michael schooling has continued to be active, and we can still approach it today. It teaches us about Ahriman's first attempts as an author: attempts of a deeply harrowing, tragic character, which naturally came to expression through the vehicle of a human being, in Nietzsche's *Anti-Christ,* his *Ecce Homo,* his autobiography, and all the annotations in *The Will to Power*—those most brilliant examples of modern literary authorship, with their often very devilish contents. Ahriman wrote them, exerting his sway over what can be subject to him as printed, earthly letters. These were Ahriman's first efforts as an author, and he will continue this work. In future we will need to be wakeful and alert so that we do not take everything we encounter as literature as being all the same in character. Human works will continue to appear, but there must be people who know that one mind in particular is training himself to become one of the most illustrious writers of the near future, and that this is Ahriman! Human hands will produce the works, but Ahriman will be their author. Just as the Evangelists once wrote down the works of those beings who inspired them from supersensible realms, so Ahriman's works will be written by human beings.

And two things will come about in the further future of humanity's evolution. Efforts will be needed to root and propagate in the earthly realm what Michael once taught predestined souls in super-earthly schools and, as far as possible, to live reverently within these insights and teachings in the Anthroposophical Society, also passing them on to those who will assemble in following incarnations until the end of the twentieth century. Then some of those who hear of these things today for the first time will return to earth—and will do so in only a short while. But in the meantime there will appear on earth numerous things written by Ahriman. And it will be the task of anthroposophists to cultivate Michael wisdom faithfully, with courageous hearts to acknowledge and propound Michael wisdom, and to see Michael's first penetration of earthly intelligence in the wielding of the spiritual Michael sword by hearts into which Michael wisdom has been inscribed. The image of Michael, in new form and figure, can be one which inspires each individual anthroposophist: Michael stands within the human heart and pins under his feet all that arises as ahrimanic authorship. This will not be an outward depiction— such as paintings from the Dominican era which often presented a fixed image of scholastic Dominicans above with their books and below heathen wisdom represented by Averroes, Avicenna and so on, who are trampled under the Scholastics' feet. One can find such paintings wherever people tried to depict Christian Scholasticism combating paganism. No, instead we will need to see this image in the spirit, to have the image of devotion to Michael who enters the world and grasps hold of intelligence on earth, and of the wakefulness needed to rise above the dazzling brilliance of Ahriman's authorship which will work throughout the whole twentieth century. He will write his works in the strangest connections, but these works will come into existence, and he is preparing his pupils for his purposes. Much is already being published today that is starting to form souls' subconscious perception, so that they reincarnate swiftly and can act as tools for Ahriman as author. He will write in all fields: philosophy, poetry, drama and narrative literature. He will write in the field of medicine, law, sociology. Ahriman will publish works in every field.

This is the situation which humanity will increasingly have to face as the end of the century draws near. Those who are somewhat younger still today will see a good deal of Ahriman's widespread authorship. We will need to be alert and awake in all fields, and nurture heartfelt enthusiasm for Michael wisdom.

My dear friends, if we can imbue ourselves with such thoughts, if we can manage to feel ourselves wholly rooted in the life of spirit in the way my comments today would urge, then we will be able to find our place in civilization as true anthroposophists. Then, perhaps, we will increasingly sense that a new impetus emanates from the Christmas Foundation Meeting at the Goetheanum, that basically a mirror is held up to the Anthroposophical Society in which it can see itself as though in a 'cosmic mirror', and that also each individual can find himself reflected there, with the karma that has led him to the Anthroposophical Society.

That is what I wanted to invoke in your hearts in these lectures, for it is to hearts that we need to speak, first and foremost. Our hearts must become Michael's helpers in conquering, in taking hold of the intelligence that has fallen from heaven to earth. Just as, in the old traditions, Michael had to trample the serpent underfoot, so now the intelligence of Michael that has become the serpent must be spiritualized. And wherever it surfaces as counter-force—not raised to spirit yet ahrimanized as intellect—we must perceive it in the right way through attentiveness of anthroposophical spirit that has been tempered in the Michaelic stance.

6. *A New Michael Age and the Battle with Ahriman*

Lecture given at the Goetheanum on 28 July 1924

In this lecture I want to elaborate on what has been said so far about inner developments in the karma of the Anthroposophical Society. We have traced events in the physical and super-physical worlds which underlie what is now trying to communicate itself to the world in anthroposophy. We know, my dear friends, that recent decades have witnessed two radical impetuses in humanity's evolution. One, which I have often mentioned, is the end of the so-called dark age at the end of the nineteenth and beginning of the twentieth century. Compared with the dark age which has passed, a new age of light has dawned. We know that this dark age culminated in the state of soul which seals our spiritual eyes to the super-sensible world. In ancient times, as we know, people in general had the capacity to gaze into the world of spirit, in a dreamlike and more or less instinctual way. It was quite impossible at this ancient stage of humanity's evolution to doubt the reality of the world of spirit. But if this condition of soul, this instinctive vision of the world of spirit, had continued, what we can call individual human intelligence could never have developed: the use of reason and understanding by each person. This is also, of course, connected with what leads us to freedom of the will—the one is inconceivable without the other. In that dull, instinctive perception of the world of spirit in ancient times, we could not have found freedom. Nor could we have developed that self-reliant thinking which can be called the use of intelligence by each individual.

Both developed together: independent, individual use of intelligence and the freedom of the human will. And for this reason, our original, instinctual vision of the world of spirit had to be hidden from human consciousness, had to darken and grow dim. All this occurred if not clearly for each individual then at least for all humanity in general. By the end of the nineteenth century this age of darkness, which veiled and hid the world of spirit but in doing so allowed the development of individual intelligence and free will, had expired. And now we are entering an era in which people must penetrate again into the reality of the world of spirit, in the ways in which this is possible.

Certainly it is clear that this new era has not begun in a very light-filled way. It seems, on the contrary, as if the first decades of the twentieth century have afflicted humanity with all the worst that it has ever previously experienced at any time in its history. But this does not negate the fact that, in general, an opportunity has entered human evolution to penetrate the light of spiritual life. It is just that, through lethargy as it were, people have perpetuated the habits implanted in them in the age of darkness, so that these habits continue to work on into the twentieth century, assuming even worse forms than before—when they were justified in the dark age of Kali Yuga—for the very reason that truth could now come into bright focus.

Now we also know that the reorientation of all humanity to a light-filled era was prepared by the beginning of the new age of Michael at the end of the 1870s. Let us for a moment consider again what it really means that the age of Michael began with the last third of the nineteenth century. Just as the three kingdoms of nature surround us in the physical and sensory world—the mineral, plant and animal kingdoms—so we should be aware that the higher realms, which we have frequently called the realms of the hierarchies, surround us in the world of spirit. Just as we descend as it were from the human being into a lower realm of nature, to the animal kingdom, so, when we ascend into the supersensible, we arrive at the realm of the Angeloi. These have the task of leading, guiding and protecting every individual person on their journey from one life on earth to the next. Thus the tasks arising for the world of spirit in relation to individual people are assigned to the beings from the realm of the angels.

If we then ascend further to the realm of the Archangeloi, we find that these have the most varied tasks. One such task, however, is to guide and oversee the fundamental tendencies of human beings in each successive age. For around three centuries, up to the end of the 70s of the nineteenth century, what we can call the rulership of Gabriel held sway. This dominion of Gabriel could be perceived by someone who penetrated the depths of human evolution—rather than, as is common today, just skimming its surface—in the fact that huge, significant impulses for humanity's development were transposed into the forces we can call those of heredity. More than in any other era, the last three centuries preceding the last third of the nineteenth century saw huge significance attributed to the forces of physical inheritance working through the generations.

This came to expression in the urgency with which people regarded the problem of heredity in the nineteenth century. People felt that their capacities of soul and spirit were dependent on heredity—as though at the last moment people started to sense what had held sway through the sixteenth, seventeenth and eighteenth centuries, and through a large part of the nineteenth century, as the impact of natural laws in human evolution.

At this time people likewise saw their mental and spiritual development as tied to the qualities inherited from parents and grandparents. All the attributes connected with physical reproduction became particularly important, and an outward sign of this, in turn, was the interest which people showed in questions of reproduction, and sexual issues in general, at the end of the nineteenth century. In the centuries referred to, the most important spiritual impulses approached humanity in a way that sought realization through physical inheritance.

The age during which Michael guides and directs humanity will stand in stark contrast to that former era. This new period, which started at the end of the 1870s, and in which we now find ourselves, will combine its impetus with what we are now also coming to know as the age of light that starts in the twentieth century. These two streams of impulse interpenetrate. Today let us first examine the real nature of a Michael age. I say 'a' Michael age, since this guidance and direction I have spoken of involves a being from the realm of the archangels taking the spiritual helm of humanity's evolution for a period of around three hundred years, in those domains and regions where civilization is chiefly focused.

As I said, Gabriel held sway in the sixteenth, seventeenth, eighteenth and nineteenth centuries, and was then relieved by Michael. There are seven such archangels who lead humanity, and thus their periods of dominion recur in a cyclical way. As we live today in this new Michael age, we have good cause to look back and recall the last age when Michael led and guided humanity. This last Michael age, which preceded the founding of Christianity and the Mystery of Golgotha, concluded at the time of the deeds of Alexander, and the establishing of Aristotelian philosophy.

If we trace all that happened in Greece and the regions surrounding it in pre-Christian times up until the time of Aristotle, for a period of three hundred years, we find ourselves in another Michael age. A Michael age is characterized by the most varied conditions, but in particular by the fact that, in a Michael age of this kind, what sets the tone are humanity's most spiritual interests, depending on the particular character and disposition of such an age. In particular, a cosmopolitan, an international character will permeate the world. National distinctions and differences cease. In the Gabriel age, in contrast, national impulses were kindled within European civilization and its American appendage.

In our Michael age these impulses will be wholly overcome over the course of three hundred years. In every Michael age humanity is generally pervaded by a universally human character in contrast to specific interests of separate nations or groups of people. At the time of the last Michael age before the Mystery of Golgotha this expressed itself in that powerful tendency arising in Greece which led to the campaigns of Alexander, in the course of which Greek culture and civilization were carried in brilliant fashion into Asia and Africa, spreading through many nations and peoples who hitherto had cultivated quite different outlooks. The extraordinary grandeur of this deed culminated in what was established in Alexandria: a cosmopolitan character which strove to give to the whole civilized world of that time the spiritual forces that had accumulated in Greece.

Such things occur under the impetus of Michael, and did so too at that time. And those who participated in these earthly deeds undertaken in the service of Michael were not on earth at the time of the Mystery of Golgotha. All those beings who belonged in the sphere of Michael, whether they were human souls who had passed into the world of spirit at death after the end of the Michael age—and thus were disembodied human souls—or those who never incarnate on earth, were all connected with each other in shared experience in the world of spirit at the time when the Mystery of Golgotha was occurring on earth.

Now we have to vividly conjure before our souls what this really means. Looking at things from the earthly perspective, we can say that humanity on earth had arrived at a certain point in its evolution. The high sun spirit Christ comes to earth, and assumes embodiment in the human being Jesus of Nazareth. The inhabitants of earth experience Christ, the high sun spirit, arriving in their midst. But they have little knowledge which would enable them to properly understand and evaluate this event.

The disembodied souls, on the other hand, who surrounded Michael and who were then living in the sun-sphere in supersensible worlds, knew with great clarity what occurred for them from the other perspective. They experienced what occurred for the world from the perspective of the sun, witnessing how Christ—who until then had been active in the realm of the sun, so that people on earth could only reach him by elevating themselves to the sun-sphere through the mysteries—took leave of the sun in order to unite with humanity on earth.

For the beings who belong to the community of Michael this was a mighty, vast event because this Michael community has a particular connection with all the cosmic destinies emanating from the sun. They had to take their leave of

Christ, who had previously dwelt in the sun, and who from then on was to take up his dwelling on earth. This is the other aspect.

But something else was simultaneously connected with this. We can only properly evaluate it if we consider the following. People in ancient times were unable to reflect or live in thoughts that push their way out from within. In some respects they were wise, infinitely wiser than modern humanity, but they were not 'clever' in the modern sense. Today we call someone clever who can produce thoughts out of himself, can think logically, bringing one thought into connection with another in a sequence, and suchlike. This was not so then. In ancient times thoughts were not created autonomously out of oneself. Instead they were sent down to people together with the revelations they received from the world of spirit. People did not reflect so much as receive spiritual content through revelation, in such a way that thoughts were contained in it. Nowadays we think and reflect about things, whereas then the thoughts came to people in soul impressions. These were inspired thoughts rather than self-directed ones. And the cosmic intelligence which in this way descended to human beings with spiritual revelations was under the sway and direction of that same spiritual being whom we call the archangel Michael, if we use Christian terminology. In the cosmos he held sway over cosmic intelligence.

We need to see what this means. People such as Alexander the Great had a clear awareness, albeit rooted in a different context of ideas, that his thoughts came to him from Michael, although a different name was used for this spiritual being. We are here using Christian terminology, but the name itself is not the important thing. A person such as Alexander the

Great saw himself as nothing other than an emissary and
instrument of Michael. The only way he could conceive
things was that Michael really acts on earth and that he,
Alexander, was the one through whom Michael acted. That
was how people saw it, and this also gave them the strength of
will to act. A thinker or philosopher of the time had the same
view: that Michael worked in him and gave him his thoughts.

Connected with this descent of Christ to earth was the fact
that Michael, with those who belonged to him, not only saw
Christ take his leave from the sun, but also above all perceived how intelligence would gradually fall away from him.
From the perspective of the sun it could be seen very clearly
at the time that people on earth would no longer receive an
influx of intelligence from without, from the world of spirit,
but that the human being would eventually have to acquire
his own intelligence within himself. This was an incisive,
significant event: to see, as it were, intelligence streaming
down towards the earth. Little by little it was no longer found
in heaven—if I may put it like this—but was allowed to pass
down to the earth.

And then, in the first Christian centuries, this came to
particular effect. We see in the first Christian centuries how
people who retained this capacity still had some sense of what
streamed down to them from supersensible revelations with
the content of intelligence. This continued until the eighth or
ninth centuries AD. Then came the great turning point when
Michael and those who belonged to him, whether they were
incarnated or not at the time, saw that human beings on earth
were beginning to be intelligent within themselves, and that
therefore cosmic intelligence could no longer be dispensed
by Michael. Michael sensed how his dominion over cosmic
intelligence faded. And below, when spirits looked down

upon the earth, they saw how from the eighth and ninth centuries onwards this age of intelligence began, and people themselves started to form their own thoughts.

Now I have described how traditions were perpetuated in certain special schools, for instance the great School of Chartres, of what, steeped in cosmic intelligence, had once been given as revelations to human beings. I have described all that was achieved in this School of Chartres, particularly in the twelfth century, and I tried to show how the task of dispensing intelligence on earth passed in particular to certain members of the Dominican order. We only have to look at the works which arose from Christian Scholasticism— from that wonderful spiritual stream which is today wholly misrepresented both by its adherents and its opponents, because its salient aspect is ignored. We need only look at how they wrestled to perceive what concepts really mean, what intelligent content really signifies for humanity and the things of the world. The great dispute between nominalism and realism developed particularly within the Dominican order. On the one side were those who saw merely names and identifiers in general concepts, while the others saw them as spiritual content made manifest in things.

The whole of Scholasticism represents the human striving for clarity about the influx of cosmic intelligence. No wonder, therefore, that the chief interest of those surrounding Michael was focused on what was developing on earth in the form of Scholasticism. In what Thomas Aquinas, and his pupils and other Scholastics asserted, we find the earthly impress of the Michael stream at that time: the dispensing of intelligence, of light-filled, spiritual intelligence.

And now this intelligence had arrived on earth, and people needed to clarify its sense and purpose. Seen from the world of spirit, it was possible to look down upon the earth and see what belongs in Michael's realm developing below, separate from Michael's dominion, at the start of the dominion of Gabriel. Initiation wisdom, Rosicrucian wisdom, as it spread then, consisted in having some clarity about these circumstances and conditions. At this time particularly, it is important to look at the way in which the earthly and the heavenly are connected. The earthly appears to have been torn loose, one can say, from the supersensible—but it is still connected. And you can see what kind of connection this is from what I have described in the last few lectures. I can only summarize and express supersensible facts in images or imaginations. They cannot be communicated through abstract concepts, but only pictorially. It is in this way I must now describe what occurred at the beginning of this era in which the consciousness soul, and with it intelligence, incorporated itself into humanity.

This was already a few centuries after Michael had witnessed what had once been cosmic intelligence arriving on the earth, in the ninth century AD. And he saw it stream on over the earth below, above all in Scholasticism. Michael then gathered those who belong in his realm into the sun-sphere, whether these were human souls who happened to be passing between death and a new life or those who belong to him and never enter human bodies for their further evolution, but who have a certain connection with humanity. You can imagine that those human souls in particular were present whom I described to you as the great teachers of Chartres. One of the most important amongst the hosts of Michael in the supersensible worlds was Alanus ab Insulis, and there, at the beginning of the fifteenth century, he had to accomplish his particular deeds.

But also all the other souls I have mentioned to you as belonging to the School of Chartres were united with those who, also passing through life between death and a new birth, had come from the Dominican order. Souls belonging to the Platonist stream were therefore inwardly united with souls from the Aristotelian stream. These souls had experienced and undergone everything in the way of Michael impulses. Many of these souls had witnessed the Mystery of Golgotha not from an earthly perspective but from the sun. At the beginning of the fifteenth century their position within the worlds of spirit was a significant one: a supersensible school—we inevitably have to use earthly expressions—arose under the leadership of Michael. For those whom he had assembled in that supersensible Michael school at the beginning of the fifteenth century, Michael himself compressed and conveyed in vast, significant outlines what had once been the Michael mystery, had been taught to initiates in the ancient Michael mysteries, and what must now change because intelligence had found its way to the earth. In supersensible worlds everything regained vitality that had once lived as Michael wisdom in the sun mysteries. In wonderful grandeur Michael summed up the Platonism which had fed into Aristotelianism and was then brought to Asia by Alexander the Great, and to Egypt. It was shown how the ancient spirituality still lived in this. All the souls who were always connected with that stream of which I have continually been speaking, who were predestined to belong to the anthroposophical movement, to form their karma in harmony with the anthroposophical movement, participated here in this supersensible schooling. Everything taught there was done so with a focus on the fact that now all that was of the nature of Michael must be developed in a different way in human evolution below on earth, through the human soul's own intelligence.

Here it was shown how, at the end of the nineteenth century, in the last third of the nineteenth century, Michael himself would once again take up his dominion on earth; how, following the cyclical eras of the other six archangels in the intervening period since the time of Alexander, a new Michael age would begin. This would be, however, a Michael age that must be different from previous ones, for in these cosmic intelligence had always come to expression in the general affairs of human beings. Now, in contrast—and this is what Michael told his pupils at the time in the super-sensible realm—something quite different would happen in the Michael age. What Michael had managed for human beings through long aeons, what he had inspired in earthly existence, had fallen away from him. He would rediscover it when he embarked on his earthly rulership again at the end of the 1870s. He would rediscover it in the form of an intelligence that has rooted itself among human beings and is for the time being bereft of spirituality, but at the same time he would rediscover it in a particular condition exposed to the greatest degree to ahrimanic powers. For at the same time that intelligence sank away to the earth the ahrimanic powers increasingly cultivated the aspiration to wrest this cosmic intelligence from Michael as it grew earthly, and to assert it in a Michael-free form on earth alone.

This was the great crisis originating at the beginning of the fifteenth century and extending to today, in which we still find ourselves and which expresses itself in the battle of Ahriman against Michael. Ahriman does all in his power to challenge Michael's dominion over the now earthly form of intelligence. Michael in turn endeavours with all the impetus he has had since his period of rulership began again in 1879 to re-exert his sway over intelligence on earth. Human evolution stood at this decisive point in the last third of the nineteenth century. What had formerly been cosmic intelligence had become earthly, and Ahriman wished to make this intelligence nothing but earthly, perpetuating it in the way initiated in the Gabriel age. Ahriman's aim was to make this intelligence entirely mundane and a matter merely of human blood relationships, of the cycle of generations, a matter of reproductive forces.

Michael made his way towards the earth. What had necessarily taken its course on earth in the intervening period so that people develop intelligence and attain freedom was something that could only be found on the earth. He had to grasp hold of it again on earth, regaining dominion over the intelligence that now works within humanity. Ahriman versus Michael, and Michael required to defend against Ahriman what the former had dispensed through aeons for the benefit of humanity. Human beings are in the midst of this battle. To be an anthroposophist means, among other things, to understand this battle at least to some extent. And it can be found everywhere. Its real form stands behind the scenes of all historical developments, but it can also be found everywhere in manifest realities.

My dear friends, the souls who were present at that time in the supersensible school of Michael participated in the teachings I have just briefly outlined to you, comprising a repetition of what had been taught in the sun mysteries since ancient times, a prophetic vision of what must occur when the new Michael age begins, and a fervent call to those surrounding Michael to pour themselves utterly into the

Michael stream, to take up these impulses so that Intelligence can be reunited with the Michael being.

These wonderful teachings full of grandeur, in that supersensible school directed by Michael himself, passed into the souls who could absorb them; and at the same time these souls took part in a mighty event that is only repeated at long intervals within the evolution of our cosmos. As I have already suggested, when we speak of the divine we point the way upwards from the earth to the supersensible world. But when passing through life between death and a new birth we really always refer back down to the earth—but not to the physical earth. In looking down like this, mighty, grandiose, divine-spiritual aspects can be seen. And precisely at this beginning of the fifteenth century, as the school I described was beginning, and numerous souls were participating in this school in the sphere of Michael, one could see at the same time something that is only repeated in cosmic evolution at long, long intervals. In looking down upon the earth one could see how Seraphim, Cherubim and Thrones—and thus the angels of the highest, of the first hierarchy—were accomplishing an extraordinary deed.

This was in the first third of the fifteenth century, the period when, behind the scenes of contemporary developments, the Rosicrucian school was founded. Normally when one gazes down to the earthly realm from the life between death and a new birth one sees the deeds of Seraphim, Cherubim and Thrones proceeding in an even, uniform way. One sees how the Seraphim, Cherubim and Thrones bear down what is spiritual from the sphere of the Exusiai, Dynamis and Kyriotetes into the physical world, and through their powers implant in the physical what is spiritual. At great intervals, what one usually sees in this way as ongoing evolution is subject to an awe-inspiring change. The last time this could be seen from the supersensible aspect was during Atlantean times. What happens in humanity at such times is perceived from the world of spirit as lightning flashes flickering through the regions of the earth and mighty claps of rolling thunder. The spirits around Michael could thus see something like a cosmic storm, while human beings on earth were as though wrapped in sleep.

Mighty things underlie what took place at the beginning of the fifteenth century in human souls. The power of this became manifest precisely as the Michael pupils were receiving their teachings in the supersensible realm. The last time such an occurrence was seen in relation to our current earthly globe was during the Atlantean period, when intelligence still remained cosmic but had taken possession of human hearts, and this manifested similarly in the discharge of spiritual lightning and thunder. Yes, that is indeed how it was. In an age which experienced earthly shocks and convulsions, in which the Rosicrucians began to spread, in which all kinds of remarkable things occurred which you can trace in history, the earth appeared surrounded by mighty lightning and thunder to spirits in the supersensible realm. This was a manifestation of the fact that the Seraphim, Cherubim and Thrones were conducting cosmic intelligence down into the nerve-sense organization of the human organism, the head organization.

Something had occurred once again here which has not yet come to full effect today, and will really only become apparent in the course of centuries and millennia: human beings are becoming utterly transformed. Previously we were heart beings. Then we became head beings. Intelligence becomes the human being's own intelligence. Seen from the supersensible realm, this is something of huge significance. From there, all the power and strength can be seen in the sphere of the first hierarchy, of Seraphim and Cherubim, who express and reveal this power and strength by bearing what is spiritual down into the physical—and not, like the Dynamis, Exusiai and Kyriotetes, only dispensing what is spiritual within the spiritual realm—and who make the spiritual into the creative principle within the physical world.

These Seraphim, Cherubim and Thrones had to accomplish deeds which, as I have said, are only repeated at intervals of long aeons. And we can say that what Michael taught those who belonged to him at that time was proclaimed below in thunder and lightning in subterranean worlds. We need to understand this, my dear friends, for this lightning and thunder should become inspired enthusiasm in the hearts, minds and souls of anthroposophists! Whoever feels a real urge to engage with anthroposophy still has in his soul (though people know nothing of this, but will eventually understand it) the ongoing resonance from absorbing that heaven-borne anthroposophy in the presence of Michael which preceded anthroposophy on earth. The teachings that Michael gave were ones that prepared what would become anthroposophy on earth.

And so we have a twofold supersensible preparation for what needs to become anthroposophy on earth: those preparations undertaken in the great, supersensible school from the fifteenth century onwards; and then what I have described to you, which unfolded in the supersensible realm as a great rite and sacrament at the end of the eighteenth and beginning of the nineteenth centuries, where the teachings received by pupils of Michael in their supersensible school assumed the form of vast pictures and imaginations. In this way souls were prepared for their descent into the physical world. Drawing on all these preparations they received the impetus to gravitate towards what would then take effect on earth as anthroposophy.

Just think of them all! The great teachers of Chartres took part in this supersensible school. As you know from what I said previously, they have not yet returned to a new incarnation, but have sent ahead those souls who chiefly worked within the Dominican order, following a kind of great conference that took place at the end of the twelfth and beginning of the thirteenth centuries. Then all these souls gathered again: those who had proclaimed ancient teachings in fiery words, and those who, in Scholasticism, in cold, clear but heart-hearkening work, had wrestled to find the sense and meaning of intelligence. All of them belonged to the hosts of Michael.

We have this school of Michael, therefore. We have the great rite of imaginal pictures, whose effects I also pointed to at the beginning of the nineteenth century. We have the significant fact that at the end of the 1870s the dominion of Michael began again; Michael, who was preparing to repossess on earth the intelligence which had fallen away from him in the intervening period. This intelligence must become Michaelic, and the meaning of the new age of Michael must be understood. Those souls who today are born with the urge for a spirituality which intrinsically contains and embodies such intelligence—as is the case in the anthroposophical movement—are those whose karma in the present age leads them in a certain sense to pay heed to what is happening at the start of the Michael age on earth. And they are connected with all those, too, who have not yet descended to incarnation again. They are connected above all with those in the Platonist stream who remained above in supersensible existence under the leadership of Bernard Sylvestris, Alanus ab Insulis and others.

But those who can today take up anthroposophy with true, inward, heartfelt devotion, who can fully connect with anthroposophy, bear within them the impetus to appear on earth at the end of the twentieth century, through what they experienced in supersensible realms at the beginning of the fifteenth and nineteenth centuries together with all the others who have not yet descended again. Until then, anthroposophical spirituality will prepare what will then need to be realized in commonality of purpose as the complete revelation of what was prepared by the streams I have referred to.

My dear friends, the anthroposophist should absorb this into his awareness, should be clear that he is already called upon to prepare the spirituality which will spread and grow increasingly until this culminates when the true anthroposophists return, and also unite with others, at the end of the twentieth century. The sincere anthroposophist should cultivate an awareness that today we need to have clear vision of the battle between Ahriman and Michael, and to participate in it. Only when a spirituality such as that which strives to flow through the anthroposophical movement unites with other spiritual streams will Michael find the impulses that can reunite him with the intelligence that has become earthly but that really belongs to him.

It still remains for me to show you the subtle means by which Ahriman is trying to prevent this, and the severity of the battle raging in this twentieth century. All these things can show us how earnest are the times we live in, and how much courage will be needed for people to take their place within spiritual streams in the right way. But by becoming aware that we can heed the call to help safeguard Michael's dominion, what I'd like to call an inner jubilation, a joyful devotion, can arise in the human soul when we realize the strength we may wield. But we have to find our way through to this mood of courageous strength, this strength of courage. Above us in letters of the spirit stand the words: 'Know that you will return before the end and at the end of the twentieth century, and that this is the time for which you have been preparing. Know how things can then take shape as you have prepared them.'

My dear friends, to know we are engaged in this battle, in this decisive conflict between Michael and Ahriman, is an intrinsic part of what we can call anthroposophical enthusiasm and inspiration.

7. Hearkening to the Voice of Karma

Extracts from a lecture given at the Goetheanum on
1 August 1924

... You see, my dear friends, one needs to know this Ahriman, or rather these hosts of Ahriman. It is not enough to despise the name of Ahriman or give a range of despicable beings this name of Ahriman. That achieves nothing. What we need to do instead is to see in Ahriman a cosmic being of the greatest imaginable intelligence, a universal being that has drawn intelligence deeply into the individual. In every way Ahriman is super-intelligent: he holds sway over a dazzling intelligence drawn from the human being as a whole—although not from the part of the human being which assumes human expression in the forehead.

... Every ahrimanic being has a huge abundance of individual intelligence, is critical in the dismissal of everything illogical, is scornful and contemptuous.

If we see Ahriman before us in this way we can also sense the absolute opposition and contrast between Ahriman and Michael. Michael is not concerned with the personal, individual aspect of intelligence. As human beings we are always exposed to the temptation to make intelligence individual and personal, according to the example of Ahriman. Ahriman really has a very dismissive view of Michael, thinking him stupid, foolish. Of course this view is in comparison with himself, because Michael does not wish to make intelligence his own personal possession, but instead wished for aeons, and still wishes, to mediate universal intelligence. And now that people have come into the faculty of intelligence they should, under his auspices, use it as something universally human, which benefits all human beings as such...

And so the battle of Ahriman against Michael rages behind the scenes. And, as I said previously, it is part of an anthroposophist's task to develop a sense of this: that the cosmos participates in this battle...

This is the impetus of Michael: now that intelligence mediated by him has come amongst us on earth, he is urging us to open the great book of nature once more and read it. Everyone who joins the anthroposophical movement should really feel that he can only understand his karma if he knows first of all that he has a personal task to read spiritually in the 'book of nature', to discover the spiritual underlying nature again... From the very beginning I have appealed to people to hearken to the voice of their karma—to hear, however subconsciously and dimly, that their karma is touched and formed by what resounds as Michael message into the world, and that they have something to do with it through their karma.

Ultimately we can see it like this: there are people who have been there, who will always be there, coming and going, and who are willing to depart from the world, in a sense, to gather together in what comprises the Anthroposophical Society. Precisely how we should understand this departure from the world and its extent and scope is another subject in itself, but it is nevertheless a kind of departure for individual souls and an entry into something different from what they originally grew from. Individual people are, after all, faced by the most varied karmic conditions. One person may find that he has to tear himself out of a context in order to unite with those who wish to cultivate the Michael message. There are some who experience their connection with the Michael message as a kind of salvation. But others may also find themselves in a position where they feel the pull towards Michael on the one hand, but also to Ahriman on the other. They may be unable to choose, feeling that life has placed them in this tug of opposites. There are some whose courage tears them out of their past context, yet who retain an outward connection with it. These are people who easily remain connected with the prevailing outward circumstances; this is certainly possible and may actually be best of all for the current state of the Anthroposophical Society. But in every instance, the people who stand within the anthroposophical movement are at odds with others who do not stand within it—including people with whom they are deeply karmically connected from past lives. So we can see the most intricate and varied karmic threads at work.

We can only understand these strange karmic connections if we recall the things we have said here about the shared experience in former lives of souls whose unconscious impulse leads them towards the anthroposophical move-ment. The great majority of these souls attended to the Michael message in the supersensible world in the fifteenth, sixteenth and seventeenth centuries, and then, at the begin-ning of the nineteenth century, participated in that mighty imaginal rite I have referred to. We can see here a great cosmic and terrestrial call invoking the karmic connections between members of the Anthroposophical Society...

8. *The Sundering of the Ways*

Extracts from a lecture given at the Goetheanum on
3 August 1924

Now let us consider the karmic circumstances of particular
individuals who approach the anthroposophical movement
out of an inner impetus. They approach it initially from the
world, for they are embedded in specific worldly contexts...
[Unlike other societies] we cannot enter the Anthroposophical Society, at least if we are absolutely honest and if
our soul is profoundly touched by it, without this having a
deep impact on our destiny. This becomes particularly clear
if we observe things with the right discernment.

Think of someone who is just joining the Anthroposophical Society or the anthroposophical movement, who
was previously connected in some way with non-anthroposophists or retains these connections... This standing
side-by-side of anthroposophical and non-anthroposophical
people is of incisive importance today. Either old karma is
resolved for the one who enters the Anthroposophical
Society or new karma begins to take shape for the one who is
not in it. These are very different things.

Let us assume that an anthroposophist stands in a close
relationship with a non-anthroposophist. This can mean that
the anthroposophist initially has old karmic connections to
resolve with the non-anthroposophist or, alternatively, that
the non-anthroposophist needs to connect karmically with
the anthroposophist for his future development. These two
kinds of instance are the only ones I have observed. Nothing

apart from such cases seems to exist. But this means that this is really a time of momentous decisions and differentiation: that either an influence is exerted on non-anthroposophists so that they approach the Michael community, or that an effect is exerted which involves this community avoiding those who do not belong to it. This is the time of great judgements and decisions, that great crisis referred to by the sacred books of all ages, which really point to the present age. The intrinsic quality of Michael impulses is in fact that they are radical and decisive and that they are becoming so precisely in our time. Those who in their present incarnation absorb the Michael impetus through anthroposophy are thereby preparing their whole being in a way that penetrates deeply into the forces which are otherwise determined merely by connections of race and nation.

Just consider for a moment how strongly one can still tell the race or nation a person belongs to. We can see that someone is Russian or French, English or German. You can tell this by looking at someone, and it's easy to pigeon-hole someone in this way, assigning him to this or that culture. We think it important to recognize whether someone is a Turk or a Russian, etc. But for those who today absorb anthroposophy with true inner power of soul, with their hearts' impetus, as their deepest life force, there will no longer be any point in such distinctions when they return to earth again. In asking where such a person hails from, you will find he can't be 'placed' in any racial group. It will seem as if he has left all such groupings behind him.

You see, at the time of Michael's last dominion, in the age of Alexander, it was a matter of spreading Greek culture in a cosmopolitan way, disseminating it everywhere. The Alexander campaign achieved a huge amount in spreading a common element and making people more equal. But this could not yet penetrate so deeply because Michael was still mediating cosmic intelligence at the time. Now intelligence has arrived on the earth. Now this impetus is taking a profound hold also on the earthly nature of human beings. The spiritual element is for the first time preparing to intervene in human life as a race-creating force. And the time will come when it will no longer be possible to say that a person looks a particular way and can therefore be assigned to a certain nation—that he's a Turk or an Arab, an Englishman, Russian or German. Instead it will have to be said that in a former life such a person felt the urge to turn to the Michaelic spirit, and that this has exerted a direct, physically creative influence on his physical form.

But this in turn is something that will have the profoundest effect on an individual's karma. And this determines the destiny of those who are sincere anthroposophists; they find it hard to come to terms with the world, yet they also feel the need to engage with the world with deep earnestness.

I have said that those who stand within the anthroposophical movement with full intensity will return again at the end of the century, and that others will then unite with them and by this means will be decided, ultimately, whether the earth and earthly civilization is saved from collapse and degeneracy. On the one hand this weighs heavily on one's heart, while on the other it is an inspiring and moving thought to recognize the mission of the anthroposophical movement. We have to focus on this mission.

But it is certainly necessary to know that anthroposophists therefore experience their karma as more difficult than others. The people who enter the Anthroposophical Society are initially predestined to experience greater difficulty in their karma than others. And if someone avoids experiencing this difficulty, wishing to have an easy karmic experience instead, this will result in a particular kind of retribution. We have to be anthroposophists also in the way we experience our karma. We have to be able to attend to our karma experience in order to be true anthroposophists. Comfortable karma, or the will to have a comfortable experience of it, will lead to retribution in the form of physical illness, accidents and suchlike.

We need to take account of the subtler, interconnected aspects of life. Then we can see various other things too. The best preparation for developing real spiritual vision is to attend to these subtler connections. It is not a good principle to try to induce in ourselves all kinds of abnormal, nebulous visionary states. But it is enormously important to concern oneself with more intimate and subtle occurrences in the threads of destiny we can observe.

Surely we can see this developing karma, my dear friends, which consists in the fact that we live or have lived alongside people who are absolutely prevented from approaching anthroposophy, despite everything which we present—or rather might present to them if they could hear it—about anthroposophy. This is our experience after all. This is something that belongs absolutely to the great arbitration and division at work in contemporary life. What happens here will be karmically significant for someone who then joins the anthroposophical movement, as much as for someone who remains outside it. This is a factor of extraordinary significance.

And now let us imagine that these people meet again in a future incarnation. What happens in a subsequent incarnation is of course prepared in the previous life. This encounter with people to whom we relate in the way I have just described will be such that the otherwise existing strangeness between people is substantially increased. Michael also works right into physical sympathies and antipathies. But this is already being prepared now, and already affects every single anthroposophist. It is therefore extremely important for anthroposophists to focus carefully on these karmic relationships which develop between himself and non-anthroposophists. Here things are at work that reach up into the next hierarchy. For you see there is a counterpart to what I have described as the race-creating impetus of Michael.

Assume that karma enables a certain individual to engage in the profoundest sense with anthroposophical impulses—with heart and soul, with soul and spirit. In this case something apparently paradoxical inevitably occurs: his angel has to learn something. And this, you see, is something of huge importance. The anthroposophical destiny that unfolds between anthroposophists and non-anthroposophists reverberates into the angelic world. This leads to a sundering of spirits in the world of the angels. The angel who accompanies the anthroposophist into his next incarnation learns to find his way more deeply into the spiritual realms than he was able to before. And the angel who belongs to the other person, who cannot gain access to anthroposophy, sinks downwards. In the destiny of the angels we can first see the great sundering happening. It is now the case—and I really want to inscribe this in your hearts my dear friends—that what was a relatively unified realm of angels is becoming a divided realm of angels, some of whom are rising upwards into higher worlds while the others are plunging downwards into deeper worlds.

While the Michael community forms here on earth, we can see above it rising and falling angels. To our consternation, when we have clearer discernment, we can actually see these streams continually...

9. The Redress of Karma

Extracts from a lecture given at the Goetheanum on
8 August 1924

... Thus, as a consequence of cosmic events, we see a split amongst the Angeloi who were formerly united with Michael. But these beings of course are involved in forming human karma. And now, if you observe everything that unfolds between death and a new birth you can see that no human soul can be left to its own devices, nor can any angel who guides human beings, but the hierarchy of the Angeloi work together, and karma unfolds in this collaboration. Now if I am connected with people in one life on earth and the consequences of this come into effect in a following life, then the angel of one person must come together with the angel of another. They must collaborate, and this is largely how things were. But then came the hugely shattering, crushing event that took place at the Ecumenical Council in 869. This gave the signal for something momentous to occur above in the world of spirit. The crushing thing that occurred to an ever-increasing extent—if one retains one's full upright power of witness in the face of such an overpowering context of facts, by making the right use of comic intelligence—was that the angel of one human soul karmically connected with another in the past did not accompany the angel of this other human soul. One of the angels of two karmically connected souls remained with Michael while the other descended to earth. What was the inevitable consequence of this? In the period between the founding of Christianity and the consciousness soul age, marked pre-eminently by the ninth century, the year 869, disorder inevitably entered human karma. This is one of the most significant things that come to expression in the history of humanity since Christ. Human karma was disrupted. In subsequent lives on earth not all experiences were properly incorporated into karma. And the chaotic aspect of recent times—which has given rise to increasing social and other kinds of chaos, cultural chaos, that cannot find its proper regulation and redress—is the disorder into which karma was brought because a split occurred within the hierarchy of angels belonging to Michael.

And now we come to something of extraordinary significance connected with the karma of the Anthroposophical Society, and which, I would say, is essential to know for acquiring the right discernment... Everything, certainly, that has led souls together in the Anthroposophical Society through an inner impetus is wholly valid. But how is it that people find their way together to share purely spiritual principles who are otherwise quite alien to each other in the world today? What are the forces which make this possible? They consist in the fact that the beginning of Michael's new dominion—the advent of the Michael age in which we live, the end of the age of Gabriel, when Michael assumes his earthly dominion—introduces the power which is to bring order back into the karma of those who have accompanied him. And thus in asking what unites the members of the Anthroposophical Society we can say that it is the fact that they are now to bring their karma into order again! If we find in the course of our life that we are entering—on the one hand—into relationships with people which do not conform to our inner impulse, which are in some way or other perhaps at odds with a right harmony in us between good and evil, and—on the other—that we nevertheless feel a continual urge to move forwards with anthroposophy, then this means that we are seeking our way back to our true karma, to fulfilling our real karma. This is the cosmic ray which the seer can perceive pouring through the anthroposophical movement: restoration of the truth of karma. And so you see this connects with a great deal of what is both the individual destiny of people in the Anthroposophical Society and the overall destiny of the whole Society. Of course these things interpenetrate.

Now we have to consider the following. The people connected with beings in the hierarchy of the Angeloi who remained in the Michael realm have difficulty in finding forms of intelligence adapted to what they need to grasp. They strive to maintain individual intelligence in a way that harmonizes with devotion to Michael. The souls whom I said participated in those preparations in the fifteenth and nineteenth centuries descend to earth with the profoundest impetus towards Michael and his sphere. Nevertheless they need to absorb individual, personal intelligence in accordance with humanity's evolutionary trajectory. This gives rise to a split in them, which needs to be resolved through spiritual development, through a convergence of individual activity with what spiritual worlds are bringing down in the present age of intelligence. The others, whose angels fell away from Michael—which is of course connected with karma, for an angel falls away if he is connected with the corresponding karma of a human being—absorb personal intelligence as a matter of course, but in them it works automatically, through their corporeality. It works in such a way that these people think, and do so cleverly, but are not

fully involved in the process. This was the great dispute
which went on for a long time between the Dominicans and
the Franciscans. The Dominicans could only elaborate the
personal intelligence principle in the most faithful possible
devotion to the Michael sphere. The Franciscans on the
other hand, the adherents of Duns Scotus—but not Scotus
Erigena—subscribed wholly to nominalism, saying that
intelligence was only a sum of words. All the debates which
took place between people at this time were really the
reflection of mighty battles between one host of Angeloi and
the other . . .

It is really true to say that one needs to seek far afield to
find the means of characterizing the grandeur of this transition at the onset of the age of Michael. We must feel ourselves embedded within these things in every aspect of the
anthroposophical movement. These great and magnificent
dimensions come to expression initially in the disorder of
human karma. If we consider how karmic connections contain a general truth and how the world is fashioned in such a
way that exceptions and anomalies can intrude even through
centuries into these general karmic conditions, and how it is
necessary to restore cosmic anomalies to their proper course,
then we will gain a sense (since this is the anthroposophical
movement's mission and task) of the great significance and
scope of the anthroposophical movement.

My dear friends, this should rest within your souls when
you remember that those who discern these things and today
feel the impetus to enter anthroposophical life will be called
on again at the end of the twentieth century to achieve the
greatest possible expansion of the anthroposophical movement at the point of its culmination. But this can only happen
if such things can live in us. There must live in us a vision of

the cosmic and spiritual forces penetrating the physical realm of earth, and likewise a knowledge of Michael's significance penetrating human perspectives.

This impetus must be the soul of anthroposophical striving. The soul itself must desire to stand fully within the anthroposophical movement. By this means we will not only be able to preserve thoughts of great scope and significance in our souls but also enliven them fully. Through such thoughts souls will be able to continue to develop in an anthroposophical way, so that the soul can really become what it ought to be, through the unconscious impetus to seek anthroposophy; and so that the soul can be imbued with the mission of anthroposophy. I have spoken these earnest words to you again, as we end, so that you can allow them to reverberate in you in peace and calm...

10. *Christ of the Elements, Christ in the Heart*

Lecture given in Torquay on 21 August 1924

In this extra hour we have been given, I'd like to add a few things to what I have already said in relation to the karma of the Anthroposophical Society. I will also elaborate on this theme again in London in a week's time.[5]

It is clear from what I have said so far that the spiritual guidance of humanity in our time is under the sway of the being whom, following Christian terminology, we call by the name of Michael. As we know, this particular rulership of spiritual life began in the 1870s, and was preceded by that of Gabriel. Now I'd like to make one or two remarks about things that are connected with this dominion of Michael.

Whenever Michael directs his impetus through humanity's evolution on earth, he is the spirit who guides the forces of the sun, spiritual sun forces, into human evolution. This is connected with the fact that we receive these sun forces into our physical and etheric body while we are awake.

Now this current rulership of Michael that has recently begun, and will last for three to four hundred years, means that the cosmic sun forces will finally and irrevocably pass over into human beings' physical and etheric bodies. And here we have to ask ourselves what kinds of forces and impulses these cosmic sun forces are.

Michael is a sun spirit first and foremost. He is therefore also the spirit who in our epoch has the particular task of substantially deepening our understanding of the truths of Christianity. We can say, in fact, that Christ comes from the sun. The sun being Christ, as I have often said, lived on earth in the body of Jesus, and since then lives in supersensible communion with the world of human beings. But humanity must gradually mature to the point where people can absorb the whole mystery connected with Christ. A substantial part of this maturation and deepening must come about during our present Michael age.

The sun forces working on earth have always been connected with an influx or wave of intellect that flows through earthly civilization. Everything we and the world possess as intellect comes from the sun. The sun is the source of all intelligence.

People today often show a certain resistance when this truth is uttered—for in fact it is quite right not to overvalue the modern form of intellect. Particularly if we connect with the life of the spirit we are unlikely to be over-impressed by modern intellectualism. This consists largely of abstract logic, and fills people today with shadowy concepts and ideas that are really very far removed from living reality. Compared to the warm, luminous life pulsing through the world and human beings, this intellect is cold, dry and sober.

But intelligence is in this state today because our intelligence, in the form it takes in the general consciousness of humanity, is only at the beginning, just as we are still only at the beginning of the Michael age. This intelligence will become something vastly different. And if we wish to gain an idea of how this intelligence will evolve in the human being we can think of how Thomas Aquinas, writing Christian philosophy of the Middle Ages, gives the appellation 'Intelligences' to the beings who inhabit the stars. In contrast to today's materialistic view we too would say that the stars are colonies of spiritual beings, wouldn't we? This strikes people today as alien: it never occurs to someone who gazes up at the stars that he is looking up at beings who have something to do with his life, and inhabit the stars just as we human beings dwell on earth.

In the Middle Ages, in the thirteenth century, Thomas Aquinas described the beings who dwell on the stars, but as a unified being—in the same way that one would speak of humanity as a single being if one observed it from a distant star. Thus he does not always say that individual beings or many beings inhabit the stars as spiritual colonies in the cosmos, but speaks of them instead as a unified star being. Nevertheless he is speaking of the intelligent beings, the intelligences, of the stars. And thus this teacher of medieval Christian doctrine, who worked in the thirteenth century, still stands within a tradition that at the time was already fading and dying away and yet still pointed clearly to the fact that everything we sum up as intelligence was once something different from what it is today.

When we look back to ancient times of humanity's evolution—I have already remarked on this in our lectures—it was not the case that people created thoughts out of themselves, that they thought about things through their own powers. This inner soul capacity of thinking, this inner capacity of forming thoughts really only fully developed from the fifteenth century, when the consciousness soul entered human evolution. And if we go back into pre-Christian times, to ancient times, people had no sense that they themselves formed their thoughts. Instead of feeling thoughts as their own possession they had the sense that thoughts were revealed to them from within things. Intelligence was a power spread out everywhere in the universe, and dwelt in things themselves. And just as we perceive colours they also perceived the intelligent content, the thought content immanent in things. The world is full of intelligence—intelligent life is everywhere. In the course of the modern era human beings have gradually appropriated it. We can say that intelligence is something spread out in the broad universe, and that in the modern era we have received a drop of it into ourselves. The drawing here depicts this:

In ancient times, in contrast, people were aware that whenever they thought, their thoughts were inspired or revealed to them. They ascribed intelligence only to the universe, not to themselves.

Through all ages the dispenser of this cosmic intelligence, which spread everywhere in the world from the sun like the radiance of light, was the spirit to whom we give the name of Michael. Michael dispenses and mediates cosmic intelligence. After the Mystery of Golgotha, in the more recent, post-Christian period, Michael's sway over intelligence gradually lapsed from and was lost to him. From the beginning of earth's evolution Michael held sway over intelligence; and when someone at the time of Alexander and Aristotle felt thoughts, that is, the content of intelligence, within him, he did not regard these thoughts as his own possession but as ideas revealed to him through the power of Michael— although at that pagan time the name given to this being was different. But gradually this content of intelligence lapsed from Michael. And when we gaze into the world of spirit we see how intelligence sank down from the sun to the earth until this process was completed by the eighth century AD. In the ninth century, as the fore-runners of subsequent thinkers, people began to develop their own, self-directed intelligence. Intelligence now becomes rooted in human souls. And Michael and his hosts look down from the sun to the earth and can say that what they dispensed and mediated through aeons has lapsed from them and has now entered human souls on earth.

My dear friends, this was the sense and mood within the Michael community on the sun. At the time of Alexander and for centuries before, Michael's previous period of dominion prevailed. At the time of the Mystery of Golgotha, however, Michael was with his hosts in the sun. And not only did they see the Christ leave the sun at the time of the Mystery of Golgotha—for they did not, as earth-dwellers did, see the Christ approaching them—but they also, at the same time, saw how their sway over intelligence gradually fell away from them.

Thus in the course of more recent human evolution, development from the Mystery of Golgotha onwards has proceeded as follows: here is the ongoing spiritual and heavenly life [red] and here the ongoing stream of earthly life [yellow]. Christ comes to the earth and henceforth evolves in union with it. The nature of intelligence gradually descends to earth until the eighth or ninth centuries [green].

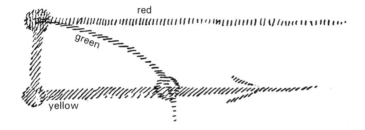

Then human beings begin to develop their own thoughts and ideas in what they call science, ascribing their thoughts to their own innate, individual intelligence. Michael gazes down and sees amongst human beings on earth what he had previously dispensed and mediated through aeons. And within the Michael community the hosts have a sense that, at their next period of dominion (beginning in the 1870s) when they again penetrate earthly civilization with their impetus, they must rediscover the intelligence which has fallen away from the heavens to earth, so as to prevail again in human souls over what they had previously dispensed from the sun, from the cosmos, through long ages.

And so, in this period, preparation is underway in the community of Michael to rediscover in human hearts what was lost and which, as it were under the influence of the Mystery of Golgotha, had made its way slowly from the heavens to the earth. I would now like to describe to you in a little more detail what form this took, how Michael and his hosts tried to reconquer in human hearts, from the beginning of the new Michael age onwards, the intelligence that had fallen away from them in the heavenly spheres of the sun. From the 1870s Michael has worked and striven for those who perceive spirit in the cosmos, and in future he aims to establish his citadel in the hearts and souls of people on earth.

This is to begin in our own age, by leading Christianity into deeper truths, so that Christ can meet with our closer understanding, can live into humanity as sun being through the sun spirit—Michael—who has always managed and dispensed intelligence. He can now no longer do so in the cosmos but aims to prevail over it again in future in human hearts.

When we find some kind of revelation of intelligence today, and wish to trace its source, we turn to the human head because, of course, intelligence, has come down to earth from the heavens, weaves within the human soul and manifests inwardly in us through the human head. It was not always like this when people sought intelligence, sought to discern what was revealed from the cosmos as intelligent creation. In former times human beings did not seek intelligence by developing the head but by seeking inspiration through the forces of the cosmos.

You can see an example of how cosmic intelligence can be sought, and was once sought but is no longer, if—as we were fortunate enough to do last Sunday—you stand in Tintagel at the place where the castle of Arthur once stood, where Arthur ruled with his twelve companions in a remarkable way that was highly significant for the European world.

Historical accounts of Arthur and his knights of the round table do not give us much of an idea of their real mission. But if you stand where the castle once stood and look with the eye of spirit on the stretch of sea visible from there, which a promontory of land divides in two [see drawing], then you can get an idea of their task. In a relatively short time you can experience a wonderful interplay of light and air, also between the elemental spirits that live in light and air. You can see how spiritual beings stream down upon the earth in

the rays of the sun, how they are mirrored in the glimmer of fleeting raindrops and reabsorb their own reflections, how what is subject to the sway of earth's gravity is animated in the air in the denser air spirits. And then you can also see, as the rain dies away and the sunrays penetrate the air's purity, how a quite different interplay of elemental spirits occurs. Here you see how sun forces work in earthly substance. When one sees all this, preferably at such an ancient site as this, one can't help feeling a sense of pagan reverence. Not so much reverence in a Christian sense, which is something different from pagan reverence. Being reverent in a pagan way means being given over heart and soul to the workings of spiritual beings in nature, to the multiplicity of spiritual beings present in natural phenomena.

Given social conditions today, people are generally unaware of these effects manifest in the interplay of natural forces. Only initiation knowledge allows us to penetrate such things. But you see, everything which is to be acquired as spiritual knowledge always has a preliminary condition and underlying foundation. In the example I gave this morning, I tried to show how perception of outer phenomena must also be enhanced by the self-correcting and harmonizing karma of two people. Likewise something particular had to be present in those times so that what was wondrously revealed and borne in from the sea could flow into the real task and mission of King Arthur and his knights.

The play of sun-illumined and sun-radiant air over the curling, foaming waves of the sea still continues to this day, as if nature were still everywhere quick with spirit over this sea and these rocky cliffs. But to grasp what was spiritually active in these natural phenomena needed more than *one* person alone. A group of people was needed, one of whom felt himself to be the central sun in their midst. His twelve companions were always taught to create in their temperaments, hearts and whole way of being a twelvefold whole, grouped as twelve individuals like the zodiac around the sun. When conferring in council, King Arthur occupied the central seat with the twelve ranged in a circle round him; and over each hung a zodiac symbol, as emblem to show under which cosmic influence they stood. It was from this place that European civilization emanated. It was here that Arthur and his twelve absorbed from the sun the forces they needed to conduct their great campaigns throughout the rest of Europe, and to drive out from people the ancient demonic powers still widespread in the European population of the time. These twelve companions, led by King Arthur, battled to secure outer civilization.

If we ask ourselves how these twelve felt, what they felt themselves to be, we can only understand the nature of their fraternity if we return to what I just characterized. People did not feel intelligence to be dwelling inside them. They did not say, 'I work out my thoughts and intelligent ideas,' but instead experienced intelligence as revelation, and sought such revelation through a group such as I described, a group of 12 or 13, together drawing in from without the intelligence they needed to form impetuses which would inform and affect civilization. And likewise they felt themselves as serving the power which we can call by the Christian and Hebrew name of Michael. The whole configuration of King Arthur's castle shows that the group of twelve under King Arthur's leadership is a Michael community, from the time when Michael still dispensed cosmic intelligence.

Yes, this community is in fact what held out longest to safeguard Michael's dominion over cosmic intelligence. And one can say that as we look out today over the ruins of Arthur's castle we can feel, preserved in the Akashic records, a sense of stones tumbling down still from what were once mighty castle gates; and as these stones fall down we can feel something like an earthly image of the lapse of intelligence, of cosmic intelligence, from the hands of Michael into the hearts and minds of human beings.

And alongside this Arthur-Michael stream, another, contrary stream arises at the place to which Christianity in more inward form had fled for refuge. This is the Grail stream, described in the legend of Parzival. In this Grail stream, too, we find twelve surrounding one figure, but now in a way that specifically takes account of the fact that intelligence, thoughts of an intelligent kind, no longer flow down from heaven to earth, but that what now flows down conducts itself in relation to earthly thoughts like the holy fool Parzival. This is what now flows down from the heavens, and intelligence is now only regarded as arising in the earthly domain.

Over here, in the north, stands Arthur's castle, where people keep the flame of cosmic intelligence alive, and desire to integrate the intelligence of the universe with earthly civilization. And on the other hand there stands, as contrast to it, the Grail castle where intelligence is no longer invoked from the heavens but where the realization has dawned that human wisdom and heavenly wisdom are worlds apart. From this other castle in the south there streams out what can pour into the intelligence that has lapsed from the heavens.

And so, if we really penetrate what was happening here we can see in these ancient times—which also reach right into the period when the Mystery of Golgotha occurs over in Asia—the most fervent efforts undertaken by the Arthur principle on the one hand to safeguard Michael's cosmic dominion over intelligence, and on the other, starting in Spain, the Grail principle with its efforts to locate intelligence on earth in future, so that it does not need to stream down from the heavens. The whole Grail legend draws its breath from the sense of what I have just expressed.

And so, by studying these two streams in relation to each other, we find the great problem which, one can say, the historical situation posed for people at this time: the continuing reverberations of the Arthur principle, and those of the Grail principle. The problem was this: how does a human being such as Parzival and, indeed, how does Michael himself find the path from the Arthurian champions, who desire to secure Michael's dominion, to the Grail champions, who wish to forge his path into human hearts and minds so that he can grasp hold of intelligence there? And then the great problem of our own age stands clear and whole before us: Michael's new dominion obliges us to grasp hold of Christianity in a deeper sense. In the two contrasting castles—the one whose ruins we can see at Tintagel, and the other castle less easily seen by human eyes because it is surrounded by 60 leagues of impenetrable forest on all sides—we find this problem inscribed in mighty form: how is Michael to kindle the impetus for grasping the truth of Christianity?

It would not be right to overlook the fact that the knights of King Arthur fought for Christ and in harmony with the

Christ impulse. But we should remember that they still sought Christ in the sun, and did not wish to give up seeking him there. Fighting their Michaelic battles for the Christ who works down in the rays of the sun is precisely what gave them the sense of carrying the heavens down to earth. In the Grail stream the Christ impetus worked in a quite different way, in full awareness that it had descended to earth and must be borne in human hearts, and unite the sun with human, earthly evolution.

During these lectures[6] I have spoken of those incisive individuals who worked in the profoundly spiritual school of Chartres in the twelfth century. I mentioned teachers there such as Bernard Sylvestris, Bernard of Chartres himself, and Alanus ab Insulis. Others were teaching there too, and had a wide group of pupils around them. In view of all I have said about the intrinsic nature of these great teachers at Chartres, we can see that they still bore within them something of the ancient traditions of living, spirit-filled nature—rather than a more materialistic and abstract view of nature. Over this school of Chartres hovered, therefore, something of that sun Christianity which the heroes of Arthur's round table, as knights of Michael, tried to send out as impulses into the world.

This school of Chartres is actually situated in a remarkable way between the northern Arthur principle and the southern Christ principle. And, like shadows cast by the Arthur castle on the one hand and the Grail castle on the other, invisible, supersensible impulses permeated the whole tone and mood—more than the content itself—of what was taught to inspired pupils in the 'auditoria' of Chartres.

This was a period when such teachers in particular represented Christianity as a manifestation of the high sun being Christ within Jesus of Nazareth. When they spoke of Christ this was simultaneously as the Christ impetus working on within earthly evolution—the Grail perspective—and as the descending sun impulse of the Arthurian stream.

From the few literary documents still extant we can no longer gain an idea of the whole spiritual perspective and underlying tone of the Chartres teachings. Reading such documents today strikes most people as little more informative than reading a glossary of names. But if we read them with spiritual insight, the brief sentences interspersing the long lists of names, terminologies and definitions show us the deeper, spiritual perspectives that these great teachers of Chartres still had.

Towards the end of the twelfth century these teachers of Chartres passed through the gate of death into the world of spirit. There they encountered that other stream, which drew on the ancient Michael period but also absolutely included Christianity—the Christ impetus which had descended from the heavens to earth. In the spiritual world they met with everything the Aristotelians had done to prepare for Christianity in ancient times through the campaigns of Alexander the Great in Asia. They also met Aristotle and Alexander themselves, who were in the world of spirit then. What these two bore in themselves could not exist on earth at that time, since it relied on abandoning a more ancient, nature-inspired form of Christianity, echoes of which still existed in the doctrines of Chartres. Something of what one can call pagan Christianity still reverberated there, in the same way that this was present at Arthur's round table. During this period of activity of the Chartres teachers, those who founded and cultivated Alexandrianism could not be on earth. Their time came somewhat later, from the thirteenth century onwards.

But in the intervening period something very significant occurred. As they passed through the gate of death, and ascended into the world of spirit, the teachers of Chartres and all who belonged to them met souls who were getting ready to descend into the physical world and whose karma predisposed them to seek out the Dominican order with its Aristotelian and Alexandrian orientation. The ascending and descending souls met. And if I am to use the shallow phrases of today, a kind of meeting and discussion took place at the end of the twelfth and beginning of the thirteenth century between those arriving in the world of spirit and those preparing to depart from it. At this meeting a great reestablishing of equilibrium occurred, through the uniting of the impulse of sun Christianity, as it manifested for example in the Grail principle,[7] and then also in the teachings of Chartres, with Aristotelianism and Alexandrianism. The followers of Alexander then descended, founding Scholasticism—whose spiritual significance is today still far from being properly valued. This school of thought adopted an extreme position to achieve what could initially only be achieved by this means: that of personal immortality in a Christian sense, which the teachers of Chartres did not propound so strongly. These latter certainly knew that we return to the lap of the gods when we pass through the gates of death, but they spoke much less of personal, individual immortality than did the Dominican Scholastics.

Many important things are connected with this. For example, when one of the Scholastic teachers descended from the world of spirit so as to spread Christianity with an Aristotelian impetus, karma meant that he was not yet able to connect fully with the deeper content of the Grail principle. This was why Wolfram von Eschenbach's version of the Grail story came about at a relatively late stage. Another soul, who descended somewhat later, brought with him what was needed, and within the Dominican order deliberations took place between an older and a younger Dominican about ways in which Aristotelianism could connect fully with a more nature-inspired Christianity, as this lived in Arthur and his knights. Then the individuals who had been Dominican teachers also returned to the world of spirit. And now that great uniting and balancing took place under the leadership of Michael himself, who gazed down on the intelligence that had come to exist on earth and gathered his hosts around him: spiritual beings of the super-earthly world, a great gathering of elemental beings and many, many discarnate human souls whose inner nature made them intent on renewing Christianity. This was not yet possible in the physical world since the time was not ripe. But a mighty supersensible centre of wisdom was established under Michael's leadership, uniting all souls who still retained a pagan streak but who longed for Christianity with those who in the first Christian centuries had lived with Christianity in their hearts in the form it then existed on earth. A Michael host formed and absorbed in supersensible regions, in the world of spirit, the Michael teachings from the ancient time of Alexander, from the time of the Grail tradition and also from impulses inherent in the Arthurian tradition.

All possible shades of Christianity lived in the souls who were drawn to this Michael community, in which teachings of the ancient mysteries and all ancient impulses of a spiritual kind were taught, but where a future orientation was also developed that pointed to the last third of the nineteenth century, when Michael would once again work on earth. All the teachings that had been developed under the leadership of Michael in the fifteenth, sixteenth and seventeenth centuries in what one can call a heavenly school would then be carried down for realization on the earth.

Now the fact that karma has united a very wide range of different souls in the anthroposophical movement, from such varying antecedents and prior circumstances, makes this movement into a Michael movement in the true sense—a movement which truly renews Christianity. This lies in the karma of the anthroposophical movement. But it also lies in the karma of many individuals who sincerely enter the Anthroposophical Society. It is the particular task of the anthroposophical movement to carry into the world this Michael impetus, which can be grasped and realized more specifically in this way. Many signs and reminders of this impetus can still be found here on earth today, for instance when one sees the wonderful play of nature around the ruins of Arthur's castle. As the centuries pass this impetus must increasingly enter civilization if the latter is not to degenerate entirely.

In the extra hour happily given us today I wanted to inscribe all this once more into your hearts.

11. The Soul of an Anthroposophist

Lecture given in London on 27 August 1924

If we trace humanity's evolution since the Mystery of Golgotha, we gain a sense that Christianity, the Christ impetus, was only able to incorporate itself into European and American civilization in opposition to certain hindrances and in connection with other spiritual streams. Indeed, the growth and gradual development of Christianity reveals the most remarkable facts.

Today I'd like to describe this development of Christianity in a few broad strokes, and relate it to what ought to live in the Anthroposophical Society—not just what ought to live within it, in fact, but what can do so. It can live there because those who feel inwardly and honestly drawn to anthroposophy will find that this urge comes to them from their inmost being.

If we give due and serious credence to the fact of repeated lives on earth, then we have to say to ourselves that everything which drives this inner impetus—which leads us to depart from the views and habits of thought of the people amidst whom we live, whose life, education and social circumstances we otherwise share, and instead seek out with others a view of the world which deeply and inwardly preoccupies us—must be due to karma arising from our former lives on earth.

Now particularly if we consider the question of karma in relation to the individuals who find their way into the anthroposophical movement, we can discover that all such individuals, really without exception, had another decisive life on earth prior to this one in the period after the Mystery of Golgotha; they have, one can say, already previously participated in the period of human evolution that follows the Mystery of Golgotha, and are now alive on earth again for the second time since then.

And now we come to the big question of how these individuals, whose karma impels them to join the anthroposophical movement, were affected by their former lives in relation to the Mystery of Golgotha.

We can discover by purely exoteric means that even people as profoundly and positively immersed in the development of Christianity as St Augustine made statements such as this: Christianity predates Christ. Before Christ came, there were Christians, although they did not yet have this name.

If we penetrate more deeply into the spiritual secrets of humanity by drawing on the science of initiation, we can wholly affirm the kind of view Augustine expresses here. What he says is true. But then a deep need arises to discover how the historical Christ impulse on earth, which came about through the Mystery of Golgotha, lived and expressed itself prior to this.

I will preface what I have to say here about this prior form of Christianity by noting that this draws on my impressions close to the place where we held our summer course in Torquay: the site in Tintagel, from which the spiritual stream of King Arthur spread. We were lucky enough to receive these impressions, still, from the magnificence of nature that once surrounded the castle of Arthur at Tintagel, the former site of the round table.

Where only the ruins of the ancient castle of Arthur are still to be seen, one can perceive, as though in thought, how stone after stone has crumbled away through the centuries, leaving scarcely anything of the ancient citadels where King Arthur and his knights once dwelt. But if one looks out to sea with spiritual gaze from the place where the castle once stood, at the water's iridescent colours and tumbling surf, if one gazes out—with a cliff on one side and the sea here—one gets a sense there of being able to absorb the elemental life of nature and the cosmos in a particularly profound way. And if we then look back through time with occult perception, if we recall the time a few millennia ago when the Arthur stream began, then we find that those who lived at the castle of Arthur—as is true of all occult sites—had especially chosen this place because they needed what unfolded there in the natural world to fulfil the impetus and task they had set themselves: for all that they were to accomplish in the world.

I cannot tell if it is always so, but my impressions there—the beautiful play of waves surging up from the depths, the wonderful crashing breakers, which are in themselves one of nature's most magnificent sights, the ocean hurling itself against the cliffs and its surf and froth swirling backwards again, the elemental spirits spiralling up from below and unfolding their activity, and sunshine pouring down from above, dancing and shimmering in the air in myriad forms— conjured in me what one can call a heathen piety. This interplay of elemental life pouring down from above and rising up from below shows the whole power of the sun, spread and unravelled before us so that we can receive it. Anyone who can absorb and hearken to what the light-born elemental beings above and the weight-born elemental beings below fuse in their interplay at the same time absorbs the power and impetus of the sun. This is different from Christian piety. Heathen piety means giving yourself up to the gods of nature who resonate, weave and work everywhere in nature's living weft.

And this whole weaving and working of nature is quite clearly what Arthur and his companions absorbed. And the significant thing here is what these people were able to receive and absorb in the first centuries after the Mystery of Golgotha.

And now my dear friends I'd like to elaborate on the special nature of this life of spirit, of human culture, at places such as that of Arthur's round table. And to do so I will need to start with a phenomenon you are all familiar with.

When we die we first leave our physical body behind us, continuing to carry our etheric body with us for a few days longer. After a few days we divest ourselves of this etheric body too, living on in the astral body and I or ego. To inner vision, a person who has passed across the threshold dissolves etherically after death. He grows ever bigger and also more diffuse, spreading and becoming ever less defined. He weaves himself into the cosmos in fact.

A strange and polar opposite evolutionary phenomenon occurred in relation to the Mystery of Golgotha. What happened when the Mystery of Golgotha was fulfilled? Until then the Christ had been a solar being: he belonged to the sun. Before the Mystery of Golgotha the knights of Arthur's round table stood high upon their cliffs and gazed out into the play of sun-born and earth-born spirits, and felt that what played in these weaving forces was penetrating their heart and above all their etheric body. In this way they absorbed the Christ impetus that was streaming away from the sun at that time, and living in everything the sun's rays brought about.

Before the Mystery of Golgotha, therefore, and spreading from Arthur's round table, the Arthurian knights took up the sun spirit—the pre-Christian Christ—into the core of their being. They sent their messengers throughout Europe to battle, purge, purify and civilize the wildness of astral bodies in the European population, for that was their task. And we can see people such as Arthur's knights of the round table migrating from this western point of what is today England and bearing what they receive from the sun across all of Europe, purging and cleansing the astrality of the very wild European population of that time—very wild at least in central Europe and northern Europe.

But then came the Mystery of Golgotha. What happened in Asia? That high solar being afterwards called the Christ had departed from the sun. This was a kind of death for Christ. Christ left the sun in the same way that we human beings leave the earth at death. Christ departed from the sun as a dying person leaves the earth. And just as someone with occult vision can perceive the etheric body of a person who dies and departs from the earth, leaving behind his physical body and divesting himself of his etheric body after three days, so Christ left behind in the sun realm what I describe in my book *Theosophy* as the Spirit Man, the seventh member of the human entelechy.

Christ 'died from the sun'; he died cosmically from the sun and descended to earth. From the moment of Golgotha onwards, one could perceive his Life Spirit on earth. After death we leave behind us the life ether, the etheric or life body. After his cosmic death, by contrast, Christ left behind him Spirit Man on the sun, and Life Spirit in the periphery of the earth. From the Mystery of Golgotha onwards, therefore, the earth was as though wrapped in the spiritual breath of Christ's Life Spirit.

Now the connections between physical locations are quite different from a spiritual perspective than they are in purely physical terms. This Life Spirit could be perceived primarily from the earthly Hibernian Mysteries, and became perceptible above all to the knights of King Arthur's round table. It was at this site, up to the Mystery of Golgotha, that the solar Christ impulse was received, and from here that it really emanated. Later the power of the Arthurian knights waned. But they stood in a living way within the Life Spirit swathing the earth in its cosmic configuration. They lived continually within this, and within this too there wove the dynamic of light and air, from the interplay of elemental beings above and elemental beings below.

If one gazes up to the high ledge on which the castle of Arthur stood, you can see the sun playing down in air and light, and the elemental beings of the earth playing upwards from below—elemental beings both above and below, sun and earth in vibrant resonance.

But in the centuries after the Mystery of Golgotha all this unfolded in the Life Spirit of Christ. As in a spiritual aura, but rooted in natural phenomena, in this interplay of sea, cliffs, air and light, the spiritual fact of the Mystery of Golgotha reverberated from this site.

Please understand what I'm saying, my dear friends. At this time, in the first, second, third, fourth and fifth centuries AD, if one gazed out over the ocean here, and was schooled in

the exercises which the twelve around Arthur practised
(which were connected with the mysteries of the zodiac) one
saw not only the play of natural forces, but it seemed as if one
could begin to read them—like having a book before you
which you can either stare at without comprehension or can
actually begin to read. A gleam of light shimmered, a wave
curled and broke, the sun glittered on an outcrop of cliff, the
sea hurled itself at the rocks: all this assumed significance as a
flowing, streaming, circling pattern, a wisdom that could be
deciphered.

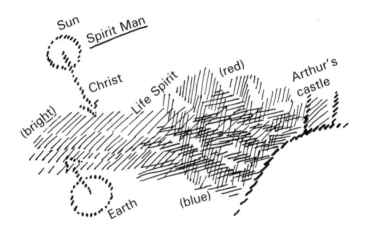

By deciphering it one could read the spiritual fact of the
Mystery of Golgotha, as all this was infused with the Life
Spirit of Christ.

   In Asia the Mystery of Golgotha had occurred, had taken
hold of human hearts and souls, deeply penetrating them and
indwelling them. If you look at the transformation that took
place in the souls of the first Christians you will find that at
the same time as what I have just described was occurring in
the west, the real Christ who had descended to earth leaving

his Spirit Man above on the sun and his Life Spirit in the atmosphere of the earth, was passing—still with his I and Spirit Self—from east to west through Greece, North Africa, Italy, Spain and over to Europe, penetrating human hearts there at the same time that he was penetrating nature here.

Thus from the west working eastwards we have the Mystery of Golgotha as something legible in nature to those who could read it, as the science, we can call it, of the more highly schooled knights of the round table. And from the east working its way westwards we have the stream—not now legible in wind and waves, in air and water, not configured in mountains and sunshine, but instead a stream radiating through the blood of human beings and their hearts, and grasping hold of their blood—which was passing from Palestine through Greece to Italy and Spain.

And so we can say that this passes through nature on the one hand and through the blood on the other, through human hearts. These two streams move towards each other: the one that still weaves within nature, that is still present today in the whole pagan stream, bearing the pre-Christian, pagan Christ, who as sun being was spread abroad before the Mystery of Golgotha by people such as the knights of the round table— but also by many others. This stream also bears the pre-Christian Christ into the world during the time of the Mystery of Golgotha. And to a large extent this all emanated from the stream we can summarize as the Arthurian. One can still encounter these things today: pagan Christianity that does not directly connect with the historical event at Golgotha.

And rising to meet this is the Christianity that connects with the Mystery of Golgotha, passing through human blood, through human hearts and souls. So we have two streams which flow towards each other: the pre-Christian Christ stream, which I will call etherealized, and the Christian Christ stream. The one later became known as the Arthur stream, while the other came to be known as the Grail stream. Both later converged; they did so within Europe and primarily also in the world of spirit.

How can we characterize this movement? The Christ who descended through the Mystery of Golgotha entered human hearts. In human hearts themselves he passed from east to west, from Palestine through Greece and Italy to Spain. Grail Christianity spread abroad through human blood, through human hearts, and Christ advanced from east to west.

This migration, as it were, was met by the spirit ether image of the Christ coming from the west, taking its impetus from the Mystery of Golgotha but still bearing within it the Christ of the sun mysteries.

A sublime and wonderful phenomenon was unfolding here behind the scenes of world history. From the west, pagan Christianity, Arthur Christianity, which also appeared under other names and in other guises, was advancing. And from the east, Christ was passing westwards in human hearts. These two converged: the actual Christ who had descended to earth encountered his image flowing towards him from west to east. This convergence and encounter occurred in 869. Until this point we have clearly differentiated a stream in the north, and passing through central Europe, that bore the Christ within it as sun hero—whether called Baldur or some other name. Under the blazon of Christ as sun hero, the Arthurian knights spread their culture.

The other stream, inwardly rooted in the heart and later becoming the Grail stream, can be found more in the south and coming from the east, and bears the true and actual

Christ within it. The stream coming from the west bears towards him what one can call a cosmic picture.

In the ninth century, then, the encounter and convergence of the Christ with himself, with his own image occurred: the Christ as brother of the human being and the Christ as sun hero, present only as image.

This characterizes the inward course of events in the first centuries after the Mystery of Golgotha, those initial centuries during which—as I have also described—the souls were present who have now once more appeared on earth and whose former lives implanted in them the sincere and authentic urge to seek out the anthroposophical movement.

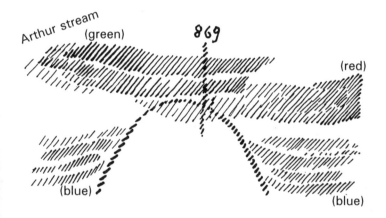

If we look at this significant Arthurian stream passing from west to east, we see how it bears the sun impulse into earthly civilization. Within this Arthurian stream there also surges and weaves what we can call in Christian terminology the Michael stream: the same Michael stream in humanity's spiritual life into which we have been entering as modern human beings since the end of the 1870s. The power we designate with the Christian name of Gabriel held sway for three to four hundred years as the guiding force in European civilization, and was then relieved in the late 1870s by the dominion of Michael. This will in turn hold sway in human culture and spiritual life, surging and weaving for three to four hundred years; and we are now in the midst of it.

At present therefore, because we stand again within the Michael stream, we have good cause to speak of movements connected with such an impetus.

We find this Michael stream if we look back to the time immediately preceding the Mystery of Golgotha, to the Arthurian stream advancing from the west in England, which was originally kindled by the Hibernian Mysteries. We can see an older form of this Michael stream if we look back to what originated centuries before the Mystery of Golgotha in northern Greece and Macedonia, and was kindled by that international, cosmopolitan stream connected with the name of Alexander the Great. This in turn was influenced by the Aristotelian world view. What occurred in pre-Christian times through Aristotle and Alexander was rooted in Michael's dominion at the time in the same way that we ourselves are now rooted. At that time, as now, the Michael impetus held sway in culture and spiritual life on earth. Whenever a Michael impetus prevails within humanity on earth, then something that has been founded and established in one particular centre of culture or spirit is spread across many peoples of the globe, into all the regions where it can penetrate.

This occurred in pre-Christian times through the campaigns of Alexander. What had been cultivated within Greek culture was spread by this means to the regions able to receive it. And if one had asked Aristotle and Alexander where the impetus in their hearts came from to spread and disseminate the spiritual life of their time, they would not have used this name but would nevertheless essentially have said: from the impulse of Michael, from the one who works as Christ's servant from the sun.

Of the various archangels who succeed each other in dominion over human culture, Michael, both at the time of Alexander and today again in our own times, belongs to the sun. The one who succeeded Michael after the Alexander era was Oriphiel, who belongs to Saturn. Anael, who succeeded him in turn, belongs to Venus. Then Zachariel held sway over European civilization in the fourth and fifth centuries, and belongs to the Jupiter sphere. Following him came Raphael, connected with the sphere of Mercury, holding sway at the time in which, in particular, a kind of culture of medical thinking flowered behind the scenes of what was unfolding as the European civilization of the time. Then came Samael, around the twelfth century. He belonged to Mars. Following this period was that of Gabriel, who belongs to the moon-sphere. And now, since the 1870s, Michael of the sun-sphere has once again come into his dominion. Thus in rhythmic succession alternates the dominion of these seven archangel beings over culture and spiritual life on earth. And if we now look back to the last era of Michael, we find this at the time of Alexander. It was embodied in the Greek civilization, which developed through centuries and was transmitted to Asia and to Africa, culminating in the culturally mighty city of Alexandria with its great heroes of the spirit.

Occult vision finds a remarkable vista here. If we look back to these few centuries before the Mystery of Golgotha, we find the same kind of stream passing eastwards from Macedonia—in other words again from west to east, but transposed further east—as the later stream of English and Irish souls likewise passing from west to east. During the time of Alexander, Michael holds sway on earth. During the time of Arthur, with Michael now working downwards from the sun, what I have described to you is borne earthwards from the sun.

But what happened later, after the Mystery of Golgotha, with the spread of the kind of Aristotelian culture and mentality that Alexander the Great carried into Asia in his military campaigns?

At the same time as Charlemagne was establishing a kind of Christian culture in Europe with his own particular stamp, Harun-al-Rashid was exerting an influence in Asia Minor. At the court of Harun-al-Rashid we see a summation of all oriental wisdom, of all the spirituality inherent in architecture, art, science, religion, literature, poetry—everything. And we see a counsellor alongside Harun-al-Rashid who, while not being initiated into all these things, was nevertheless an initiate in ancient times, in former lives on earth. And embodied in these two—Harun-al-Rashid and his counsellor—we see transplanted to Asia a very altered form of the Aristotelianism which Aristotle derived from ancient nature wisdom. We see Alexandrian Aristotelianism permeated and impregnated with Arabism, Islam, at the court of Harun-al-Rashid.

And then we see carried over into the development of Christianity what emanated from Harun-al-Rashid, from Arabism: a kind of Arabism which one can say was retrospectively implanted into Christianity, passing through Greece but particularly North Africa, through Italy and Spain.

But before this occurred, Harun-al-Rashid and his counsellor passed over the threshold. From the life they now led between death and a new birth above the earthly sphere, they looked down upon the expeditions of the Muslim Moors to Spain, tracing from the world of spirit the path now pursued by what they themselves had cultivated and what their successors were now spreading. From the world of spirit Harun-al-Rashid focused largely on Greece, Italy, Spain, while his counsellor turned his gaze chiefly to what was spreading from the East through the regions north of the Black Sea, through Russia to central Europe.

And now we must ask: what happened to Alexander and Aristotle themselves? They were both deeply connected with the dominion of Michael, but were not incarnated on earth at the time the Mystery of Golgotha occurred.

Now we must vividly conjure the two opposite images: human beings on earth at the time of the Mystery of Golgotha when Christ becomes a human being and passes through the Mystery of Golgotha, living from then on in the earth's sphere. How are conditions on the sun at that time? The souls belonging to Michael dwell there, living in the sphere of Michael. They look out from the sun and see Christ departing from it. On earth are those who perceive Christ drawing near, while on the sun are souls who observe Christ's departure. They see him descend to the earth. This is the contrast. And this is experienced primarily by those who have participated, in their earthly lives, in Michael's dominion at the time of Alexander. They experience, as it were, the reversed Christ event: the departure of Christ from the sun. They continue their existence—I don't wish to mention various unimportant incarnations here—and in the world of spirit they experience the era of the ninth century, around 869, which is of great significance for the earthly world. At this point occurs what I just referred to: the encounter of Christ with his own image, his Life Spirit, with what was still present of the pre-Christian, pagan Christ. But an after-death encounter also took place of the two individualities who lived formerly in Alexander the Great and Aristotle with the two individualities who had lived in Harun-al-Rashid and his counsellor. Muslim Aristotelianism from Asia, as it came to expression in Harun-al-Rashid and his counsellor, encountered Alexander and Aristotle in the world of spirit. The first was Aristotelianism and Alexandrianism which had absorbed Islam, while the other was true Aristotelianism, and not subsequent teachings diluted by their passage through others. Aristotle and Alexander had observed the Mystery of Golgotha from the sun.

And now there took place the great gathering and encounter, what one can call a heavenly council, between Mohammedanized Aristotelianism and Christianized Aristotelianism—but Christianized in the world of spirit.

And thus we can say that here in the world which directly adjoins our physical earth Alexander and Aristotle met with Harun-al-Rashid and his counsellor to consult with each other about further developments in the Christianization of Europe, and point to what must come about at the end of the nineteenth century and in the twentieth century when Michael would once again hold sway on earth.

And all this unfolded as though illumined by this event of Christ's encounter with his image, standing as it were under its influence and impression. Human spiritual life was projected with great intensity into the world of spirit directly adjoining this earthly world, was engraved in it, one can say.

And below on earth there gathered the eighth Ecumenical Council of Church Fathers in Constantinople, which formulated the dogma that the human being did not consist of body, soul and spirit but only of body and soul, and that the soul merely possessed certain spiritual attributes. The teaching of trichotomy—the name given to the teaching of a threefold body, soul and spirit—was abolished. Anyone who continued to profess this teaching in Europe became a heretic. The Christian Fathers in Europe absolutely avoided speaking of the trichotomy, of body, soul and spirit, and referred only to the body and soul.

The decisive event I have described, which occurred in supersensible worlds in 869 AD, cast its shadow down into the world. The dark age of Kali Yuga found in it a particular impetus, while above, over it, there unfolded what I have described.

This was the real course of events: in the physical world, the Council of Constantinople at which the spirit was abolished; and in the world immediately adjoining the physical world, a heavenly council coinciding with the encounter of Christ with his image.

But it was clear that it was necessary to wait until the new Michael dominion began. Yet teachers repeatedly appeared who knew something, though in somewhat decadent form, of what was really going on behind the scenes of earthly existence. There were teachers able to depict the spiritual content of the world—all that informs the world of spirit in the world directly adjoining the physical world—even if not in very accurate pictures. And such teachers sometimes found willing ears. And such ears belonged to people who in this way heard something of Christianity, although only in the odd intimation here and there—heard something of what was to come in the twentieth century after Michael's dominion had begun again.

You yourselves, my dear friends, have within you the souls of these people who were incarnated at the time and listened to others who spoke of the forthcoming era of Michael's dominion, under the influence of the impetus streaming to them from that heavenly council I spoke of.

From such an experience in a former life, in the first centuries AD—not in the ninth century but prior to this and subsequently—developed the unconscious urge, once Michael's dominion should come at the end of the nineteenth century and the beginning of the twentieth, to gaze upon the place where spiritual life is truly to be cultivated again under the influence of Michael. This implanted itself in the souls of those who heard the teachings which contained something of the secrets we have spoken of today.

Thus was implanted in souls a longing to seek out the Christianity which anthroposophy would spread under the dominion of Michael at the end of the nineteenth and beginning of the twentieth century. And what these souls experienced at the time comes to expression now in a new incarnation in the fact that certain souls find their way to the anthroposophical movement.

Teachings which link to a kind of confluence of ancient, pre-Christian, cosmic Christianity and inner Christian teachings, which link to the spirit living and weaving in nature and yet can also connect with the Mystery of Golgotha, were now taught on earth at the time when the souls who now feel strongly drawn to anthroposophy had passed over the threshold once more and were living between death and a new birth, and in some cases descending to incarnation again on earth. We can see how the ancient teachings, which still regarded Christianity in a cosmic way, continued to survive on earth, cultivating the traditions of the ancient mysteries. We can see such teachings propagated further by significant schools in Europe, such as the School of Chartres in particular in the twelfth century, where important teachers such as Bernard Sylvestris, Alanus ab Insulis and other great teachers taught. We see how these teachers lived and worked in such figures as for example Brunetto Latini, whom I mentioned recently. Brunetto Latini, the great teacher of Dante, bore such teachings within him. In this way we see a further propagation of what still embodied a connection between cosmic Christianity and the purely human, earthly Christianity, which increasingly came to predominate on earth.

The Council of Constantinople held on earth was an earthly shadow or counter-image of something that was taking place in the world of spirit. A continual connection existed between what was happening in the world directly bordering on the physical world, and what was happening in this physical world itself. The most important teachers of Chartres felt inspired by the real Alexander and the real Aristotle, but also in the most powerful way by Plato and by everything in medieval mysticism which hearkened back to Plato and Neoplatonism.

And now something of great significance occurred. The people who gathered most closely around Michael, who had largely therefore been incarnated at the time of Alexander, were now dwelling in the world of spirit. They gazed down with some interest to see how Christianity was developing under the teachers of Chartres. However they waited until these teachers, who were the last to teach cosmic Christianity, rose into the world of spirit. And at the end of the twelfth and beginning of the thirteenth century, the teachers of Chartres, who were more strongly informed by Platonism, met in the supersensible sphere adjoining the earth with those who had been present at the heavenly council in 869. A kind of meeting took place, since we must use earthly words for such an exalted event, between those teachers of Chartres now rising into the world of spirit and preparing to continue their development there, and the others who were preparing to descend, and who included the individualities of Alexander and Aristotle themselves, who directly afterwards incarnated and subsequently became members of the Dominican order. And on earth there developed Scholasticism, which is nowadays so disregarded although it would be very important for us to perceive its deeper significance. In what now appeared as Scholasticism on earth the preparation took place for all that was to occur later in the new Michael age.

In order to live their way fully into Christianity and to stand wholly within it, souls incarnated who belonged to the sphere of Michael, and who had formerly been living at the time of Alexander. These had not participated in the first Christian centuries, or had only done so in fairly unimportant incarnations. These souls now incarnated in order to live fully into Christianity in the Dominican order or in other Christian monastic orders, but primarily the Dominican order. Then they passed through the gate of death and entered the world of spirit, and continued to work there.

In the fifteenth century, and this lasted on into the sixteenth century too—but we must remember that temporal relationships are quite different in the world of spirit—the great schooling took place in the supersensible realm which Michael himself conducted for those gathered around him. A supersensible or spiritual school was established in which

Michael himself was the teacher, and in which those souls participated who were at that time inspired in particular by the former Michael age, and by their immersion in Christianity in the way I described. All the disembodied human souls belonging to Michael participated in that great school which took place in the fifteenth and sixteenth centuries in the supersensible realm. All the beings from the hierarchies of the angels, archangels and archai who belonged to the Michael stream also took part. Numerous elemental spirits took part as well.

And here all ancient Mystery teachings were recalled in a wonderful vista, giving the souls detailed knowledge and insight into the nature of these ancient mysteries. Their gaze was directed back to the sun mysteries, and those of the other planets. But a vista of the future was also revealed—of what was to begin in the new age of Michael at the end of the nineteenth century and beyond, the time in which we now stand. All this passed through these souls, and they were the same ones who now, in our age of Michael, feel deeply drawn to the anthroposophical movement.

In the meantime, on earth, the last bout of the struggle was taking place. Harun-al-Rashid incarnated again, and in this new incarnation established the impetus for materialism as Lord Bacon of Verulam. The universality in Bacon's teachings comes directly from Harun-al-Rashid, as does all that lived in Bacon as intellectualism and materialism. Bacon reappeared as a reincarnation of Harun-al-Rashid. His counsellor, who pursued the other direction, reappeared in the same period as Amos Comenius.

And thus we see that while Christianity infused with Aristotelianism underwent its major development in the fourteenth, fifteenth, sixteenth and seventeenth centuries, materialism was at the same time established in human culture on earth in the science of Bacon, the reincarnated Harun-al-Rashid, and was likewise established in the field of education under the influence of Amos Comenius, the reincarnated counsellor of Harun-al-Rashid. Both these figures worked together.

Amos Comenius and Bacon both gave rise to something strange in the world of spirit when they passed over again into death. When Bacon of Verulam crossed the threshold, one could see a whole world of idolatrous figures, demonic idols emanating from his etheric body, due to the particular mode of thinking he had acquired in his incarnation as Bacon. These infused the world of spirit where, amongst the souls whom Michael had been teaching, there still resonated the after-effects of that heavenly council. In this world of spirit these idols spread abroad.

As my first Mystery play tried to show, what happens on earth has powerful effects that resonate into the world of spirit. Bacon's earthly mentality had a tumultuous effect upon the world of spirit, engendering a whole world of idolatrous demons there.

And the kind of materialistic education which Amos Comenius established on earth provided as it were the foundation, the world, the habitable sphere or universal atmosphere for Bacon's idols. One can say that Bacon provided the idols while Amos Comenius supplied the other 'kingdoms' surrounding them through what he had established on earth. Just as we have the mineral, plant and animal kingdoms around us, these idols of Bacon had the other kingdoms which they needed.

And the task of battling all this, these demonic idols, now fell to the individuals who had once followed the lead of

Alexander and Aristotle on earth. This conflict continued up to the moment when the French Revolution occurred.

The demonic idols or idolatrous demons who were not vanquished and who, as it were, escaped intact, descended to earth and inspired nineteenth-century materialism and all that ensued from it. These forces were the inspiration behind nineteenth-century materialism!

The souls who remained behind, who with the help of the individualities of Aristotle and Alexander had benefited from the teachings of Michael, came to earth again at the beginning of the twentieth century bearing in them the impulses I have described.

We can recognize many of these souls in those who come towards the anthroposophical movement. This is the karma of those who approach the anthroposophical movement authentically, with inner sincerity.

It is a shattering experience to perceive what directly underlies outer events at the present time. Yet, with the guiding influence of the Goetheanum Christmas impetus, this must resonate downwards into the souls and the hearts of those who call themselves anthroposophists. It is something that needs to live in the hearts and souls of anthroposophists. And it will give us the strength to continue our work, for those who are anthroposophists in the honest and authentic sense will feel a strong impetus to return to the earth soon. And prophecies connected with Michael tell us that numerous anthroposophists will come to earth again around the end of the twentieth century so as to bring to its full culmination what is founded and established with all strength today as the anthroposophical movement.

The following thought is what should really move and give impetus to the souls of anthroposophists:

I stand here, and the anthroposophical impulse is in me. I recognize it as the Michael impulse. I am waiting, and strengthening myself for my waiting by undertaking true anthroposophical work in the present, and using the brief intervening period accorded anthroposophists' souls in the twentieth century between death and a new birth, so as to return again at the end of the twentieth century and continue this movement with far greater spiritual strength. I am preparing myself for this new age, at the transition from the twentieth to the twenty-first century, for many destructive forces are at work on the earth. All cultural life, all civilized life on earth must descend into decadence if the spirituality of the Michael impetus does not take hold of human beings, and if they do not, in turn, become able to raise and elevate once more a civilization that is teetering on the brink.

Such thoughts are those of a true anthroposophical soul. If such authentic souls, such honest anthroposophists can be found, who wish in this way to bear spirituality into earthly life, then an upward movement and dynamic will arise. If such souls do not appear, then decadence will take its inexorable downward course. The world war, with all the evil attendant on it, will be just the beginning of still greater evil. Today humanity stands before a great crisis: either it will see all civilization collapsing into the abyss or else spirituality will raise civilization up by the power of the Michael impetus, through which the Christ impetus works, thus continuing, enriching and sustaining it.

My dear friends, these are the thoughts I needed to impress on you, and I hope that they will continue to resonate in your souls. As I have often said when concluding a joyous and fulfilling time in which we have talked and worked together, we can take it as our karma that we come together like this in physical immediacy, yet we also remain united when, physically, we go our separate ways. Let us remain united in the signs that reveal themselves to our spiritual eyes, our spiritual ears if we hearken earnestly to what, if you have properly understood me, I hope has flowed towards you in these lectures.

Postscript: The Work of the Future

Excerpt from Rudolf Steiner's Last Address, given at the
Goetheanum on 28 September 1924

... When we read the *Fragments* by Novalis and attend profoundly to the abundant life in them, we will find that they
make such a deep impression on us because what lives in
Novalis's soul lends a magical idealism, an almost divine,
poetic glory to everything our eyes perceive in immediate
sensory reality and recognize as beautiful. He knows how to
resurrect the most ordinary material thing in shining spiritual
light through his magical, poetic idealism.

And so, my dear friends, we can see in Novalis a radiant
and splendid herald of that Michael stream which should
guide all of you—both now while you are alive and later when
you pass through the gate of death. In the world of spirit you
will rediscover all those I have spoken of. You will find all
those with whom you need to prepare the work that is to be
accomplished at the end of this century, which is to lead
humanity out of the great crisis in which it now finds itself.

This work is to wholly and powerfully infuse and penetrate
life with the strength and will of Michael—nothing other than
the forerunner of Christ's will and strength—which strives to
implant this Christ force into earthly life in the right way.
Only if this Michael power can really vanquish all that is
dragon- and demon-like, which you are also very familiar
with, and if all of you take up the Michael thought in this way,
in the light, if you take up this Michael thought with faithful
hearts and in inward love, and sustain it there, if you try to

take the sacred mood of Michael kindled this year as your new impetus for what can not only reveal this Michael thought intensely in your soul but can also give life to it in your deeds, then you will be the true servants of this Michael thought. Then you will be worthy helpers of the Michaelic force that is to unfold in Earth evolution through anthroposophy.

If the Michael thought begins to live vibrantly and fully in the near future in four times twelve human beings—who are acknowledged as such not by themselves but by the Goetheanum leadership—and if these four times twelve human beings become leaders who spearhead a celebratory mood of Michael, a real festival of Michael, then we will be able to gaze upon the light radiating from the Michael stream and Michael activity in the humanity of the future.

To emphasize this, my dear friends, I have made the effort to briefly gather my strength today, so as to be able at least to speak these words to you. For now my force is spent and I can say no more. But I wanted these words to speak to your souls, to urge you to take up the Michael thought in the way that only a heart faithful to Michael can when it looks upon Michael clad in the bright rays of the sun, to Michael who points to what needs to happen for this Michael garment, this garment of light, to become the cosmic words which are also the words of Christ: the cosmic words that can transform the cosmic logos into the logos of humanity. My words to you today therefore are these:

> Spiritual powers springing from
> sun-forces: shining, world-grace bestowing:
> divine, creative thinking destines you
> to be Michael's dress of rays.

He, the messenger of Christ, endows you with
Holy cosmic will, sustaining us;
You, the bright beings of ether worlds,
Bear to human beings the word of Christ.

So appears the Christ proclaimer
to patient, longing, thirsting souls:
for them your shining word streams onwards
into the future age of spirit man.

You, pupils of spirit knowledge,
take up Michael's wise direction,
take up the loving word of cosmic will
actively into your striving souls.

Notes

1. See *World History in the Light of Anthroposophy*, Rudolf Steiner Press, 1977.
2. St Augustine, in: *Retractiones*, I.xiii.3.
3. There is a play on words here, as *Kante* means 'edge' or 'angle' in German.
4. Maurice Maeterlinck: *Le Grand Secret*, Bibliotheque Charpentier, 1921.
5. See next lecture.
6. Published in English as: *True and False Paths in Spiritual Investigation*, Rudolf Steiner Press, 1985.
7. Translator's note: Although 'Grail principle' is given in the German source text, 'Arthurian principle' would seem to make more sense here.

Sources

Prelude: Lecture extract of 4 July 1924, Dornach, in GA 237, Volume III of: *Esoterische Betrachtungen karmischer Zusammenhänge*. English translation in *Karmic Relationships*, Volume III, Rudolf Steiner Press 1977.

1: Lecture of 6 July 1924, Dornach, in GA 237, Volume III of: *Esoterische Betrachtungen karmischer Zusammenhänge*. English translation in *Karmic Relationships*, Volume III, Rudolf Steiner Press 1977.

2: Lecture of 8 July 1924, Dornach, in GA 237, Volume III of: *Esoterische Betrachtungen karmischer Zusammenhänge*. English translation in *Karmic Relationships*, Volume III, Rudolf Steiner Press 1977.

3: Lecture of 18 July 1924, Arnhem, in GA 240, Volume VI of: *Esoterische Betrachtungen karmischer Zusammenhänge*. English translation in *Karmic Relationships*, Volume VI, Rudolf Steiner Press 1971.

4: Lecture of 19 July 1924, Arnhem, in GA 240, Volume VI of: *Esoterische Betrachtungen karmischer Zusammenhänge*. English translation in *Karmic Relationships*, Volume VI, Rudolf Steiner Press 1971.

5: Lecture of 20 July 1924, Arnhem, in GA 240, Volume VI of: *Esoterische Betrachtungen karmischer Zusammenhänge*. English translation in *Karmic Relationships*, Volume VI, Rudolf Steiner Press 1971.

6: Lecture of 28 July 1924, Dornach, in GA 237, Volume VI of: *Esoterische Betrachtungen karmischer Zusammenhänge*. English translation in *Karmic Relationships*, Volume III, Rudolf Steiner Press 1977.

7: Lecture extract of 1 August 1924, Dornach, in GA 237, Volume III of: *Esoterische Betrachtungen karmischer Zusammenhänge*. English translation in *Karmic Relationships*, Volume III, Rudolf Steiner Press 1977.

8: Lecture extract of 3 August 1924, Dornach, in GA 237, Volume III of: *Esoterische Betrachtungen karmischer Zusammenhänge*. English translation in *Karmic Relationships*, Volume III, Rudolf Steiner Press 1977.

9: Lecture extract of 8 August 1924, Dornach, in GA 237, Volume III of: *Esoterische Betrachtungen karmischer Zusammenhänge*. English translation in *Karmic Relationships*, Volume III, Rudolf Steiner Press 1977.

10: Lecture of 21 August 1924, Torquay, in GA 240, Volume VI of: *Esoterische Betrachtungen karmischer Zusammenhänge*. English translation in *Karmic Relationships*, Volume VIII, Rudolf Steiner Press 1975.

11: Lecture of 27 August 1924, London, in GA 240, Volume VI of: *Esoterische Betrachtungen karmischer Zusammenhänge*. English translation in *Karmic Relationships*, Volume VIII, Rudolf Steiner Press 1975.

Postscript: Lecture extract of 28 September 1924, Dornach, in GA 238, Volume IV of: *Esoterische Betrachtungen karmischer Zusammenhänge*. English translation in *Karmic Relationships*, Volume IV, Rudolf Steiner Press 1997.

Further Reading

All by Rudolf Steiner:

Karmic Relationships, Vols. 1–8
Manifestations of Karma
Reincarnation and Karma
An Exercise for Karmic Insight (printed book and audio book available)

Anthroposophical Leading Thoughts
The Anthroposophic Movement
The Christmas Conference for the Foundation of the General Anthroposophical Society 1923/24
The Foundation Stone Meditation

Available via Rudolf Steiner Press (UK),
www.rudolfsteinerpress.com and SteinerBooks (USA),
www.steinerbooks.org

Note on Rudolf Steiner's Lectures

The lectures and addresses contained in this volume have been translated from the German, which is based on stenographic and other recorded texts that were in most cases never seen or revised by the lecturer. Hence, due to human errors in hearing and transcription, they may contain mistakes and faulty passages. Every effort has been made to ensure that this is not the case. Some of the lectures were given to audiences more familiar with anthroposophy; these are the so-called 'private' or 'members' lectures. Other lectures, like the written works, were intended for the general public. The difference between these, as Rudolf Steiner indicates in his *Autobiography*, is twofold. On the one hand, the members' lectures take for granted a background in and commitment to anthroposophy; in the public lectures this was not the case. At the same time, the members' lectures address the concerns and dilemmas of the members, while the public work arises from, and directly addresses Steiner's own understanding of universal needs. Nevertheless, as Rudolf Steiner stresses: 'Nothing was ever said that was not solely the result of my direct experience of the growing content of anthroposophy. There was never any question of concessions to the prejudices and preferences of the members. Whoever reads these privately printed lectures can take them to represent anthroposophy in the fullest sense. Thus it was possible without hesitation—when the complaints in this direction became too persistent—to depart from the custom of circulating this material "For members only". But it must be borne in mind that faulty passages do occur in these reports not revised by myself.' Earlier in the same chapter, he states: 'Had I been able to correct them [*the private lectures*], the restriction *for members only* would have been unnecessary from the beginning.' The original German editions on which this text is based were published by Rudolf

Steiner Verlag, Dornach, Switzerland in the collected edition (*Gesamtausgabe*, 'GA') of Rudolf Steiner's work. All publications are edited by the Rudolf Steiner Nachlassverwaltung (estate), which wholly owns both Rudolf Steiner Verlag and the Rudolf Steiner Archive.